Cracking the Human Resource (HR) Interview:

100 Top Questions & Answers

Copyright © 2023 by GREESHMA AGC

With each chapter dedicated to a specific topic, "Cracking the Human Resource (HR) Interview: 100 Top Questions & Answers" is your comprehensive companion to conquering the multifaceted challenges of HR interview. Whether you are a HR seeking to enhance your skills or a candidate preparing for diverse scenarios, this guide is your definitive resource for success in HR interviews.

However, the author and publisher disclaim any liability for any loss or risk that may be incurred as a consequence of the use and application of the contents of this book.

Cover design by Eva Mariam.

Embark on a transformative journey in your Human Resource (HR) career with our definitive guide – "Cracking the Human Resource (HR) Interview: 100 Top Questions & Answers."

Unlock the Gateway to HR Interview Success in multinational companies.

In-Depth Question Coverage: Navigate through a comprehensive collection of 100 top questions covering every crucial aspect of the HR domain.

Strategic Insights: Gain strategic insights into Recruitment and Talent Acquisition, Performance Management, Training and Development, HR Policies, and Compliance. Stay ahead of the curve with the latest trends.

Expertly Crafted Answers: Our answers go beyond the surface, offering nuanced insights backed by industry expertise. Learn how to articulate your thoughts and stand out in HR interviews.

Real-world Scenarios: Tackle scenario-based questions that mirror the challenges HR professionals face daily. Develop problem-solving skills and enhance your decision-making capabilities.

Career Advancement Strategies: Elevate your HR career with tips on effective leadership, collaboration, and professional development. Stay informed about the latest HR technology and analytics.

Global HR Management: Acquire a global perspective on HR challenges and solutions, ensuring you are equipped for success in the diverse and dynamic world of HR.

Why "Cracking the HR Interview"?

Holistic Question Coverage: A well-rounded guide covering a spectrum of HR topics ensures you are well-prepared for any interview scenario.

Real-world Application: Navigate through real-world scenarios to enhance your problem-solving skills and make informed decisions in challenging situations.

Strategic Mastery: Learn to approach HR strategically, staying updated with industry trends and leveraging technology for effective HR practices.

Career Transformation: Whether you are a seasoned professional or a newcomer, this guide provides insights that can catapult your HR career to new heights.

Seize the opportunity to excel in your HR interviews – grab your copy of "Cracking the HR Interview" now and position yourself for success in the competitive realm of Human Resources!

Table of Contents

General HR Knowledge

Answer

Human Resources (HR) managers are responsible for managing the overall administrative tasks related to human resources in an organization.

They ensure compliance with employment laws and regulations, develop and implement HR policies and procedures, and oversee recruitment, hiring, and training processes.

HR managers also handle employee relations, including resolving conflicts and addressing employee concerns.

They may be involved in performance management, compensation and benefits administration, and employee development and training programs.

HR managers are often responsible for maintaining employee records and managing payroll processes.

They may also be involved in strategic HR planning and forecasting to meet the organization's workforce needs.

Real-world examples of HR managers' responsibilities include:

- Developing and implementing a recruitment strategy to attract and hire top talent.
- Resolving conflicts between employees to maintain a positive work environment.
- Conducting training programs to enhance employees' skills and knowledge.
- Managing the payroll process to ensure accurate and timely payment of employees.

To summarize, HR managers are responsible for managing various aspects of human resources, from recruitment to employee relations and strategic planning. They ensure compliance with employment laws, develop HR policies, and support the overall growth and development of the organization's workforce.

Can you explain the role of an HR Manager in an organization?

Answer

The role of an HR Manager in an organization is to oversee and manage all aspects of the company's human resources activities. They are responsible for developing and implementing HR strategies and policies that align with the organization's goals and objectives. Here are some key responsibilities of an HR Manager:

- **Recruitment and Selection**: HR Managers are responsible for attracting and hiring qualified candidates for open positions within the organization. They develop job descriptions, advertise job openings, screen resumes, conduct interviews, and make hiring decisions.

- **Employee Training and Development**: HR Managers are in charge of creating and implementing training programs to enhance the skills and knowledge of employees. They identify training needs, design training materials, coordinate training sessions, and evaluate the effectiveness of training programs.
- **Performance Management**: HR Managers develop and implement performance management systems to evaluate employee performance and provide feedback. They set performance goals, conduct performance appraisals, and assist employees in improving their performance.
- **Compensation and Benefits**: HR Managers are responsible for designing and administering compensation and benefits programs to attract and retain employees. They conduct salary surveys, develop pay structures, administer employee benefits, and ensure compliance with labor laws.
- **Employee Relations**: HR Managers act as a liaison between employees and management. They handle employee grievances, mediate conflicts, and promote positive employee relations. They also ensure compliance with labor laws and company policies.
- **HR Administration**: HR Managers oversee various administrative tasks, such as maintaining employee records, processing payroll, managing employee databases, and ensuring compliance with employment laws and regulations.
- **HR Strategy and Planning**: HR Managers contribute to the development and implementation of HR strategies and plans that support the organization's overall business objectives. They analyze HR metrics to identify trends and make data-driven decisions.

By effectively fulfilling these responsibilities, an HR Manager plays a crucial role in ensuring the organization has a skilled and engaged workforce that can contribute to its success.

How do you stay updated on HR laws and regulations?

Answer

Read HR publications and newsletters: I regularly subscribe to HR publications and newsletters to stay updated on the latest HR laws and regulations. These publications provide in-depth analysis and interpretation of new and existing laws, as well as practical advice on compliance.

Attend HR conferences and seminars: I make it a priority to attend HR conferences and seminars, where industry experts and legal professionals discuss the latest developments in HR laws and regulations. These events often include workshops and panel discussions that provide valuable insights and practical guidance.

Participate in professional HR associations: I am an active member of professional HR associations, such as the Society for Human Resource Management (SHRM). These associations offer resources, webinars, and forums where members can discuss and learn about HR laws and regulations.

Collaborate with legal counsel: I work closely with legal counsel to ensure that our HR policies and practices comply with the latest laws and regulations. This collaboration helps me stay updated on any changes or updates in the legal landscape.

Network with other HR professionals: I actively network with other HR professionals, both within and outside of my organization. By sharing best practices and discussing challenges, we stay informed about any changes in HR laws and regulations that may affect our respective organizations.

What HR software and tools are you familiar with?

Answer

I am familiar with a variety of HR software and tools that are commonly used in the industry. Some of the tools and software that I am experienced with include:

- **Human Resource Information System (HRIS)**: HRIS is a software that allows HR departments to manage and streamline their HR processes. It typically includes features such as employee data management, payroll processing, benefits administration, and performance management.
- **Applicant Tracking System (ATS)**: ATS is a software that helps HR departments manage the recruitment process. It allows them to track and manage job applications, screen candidates, schedule interviews, and collaborate with hiring managers.
- **Performance Management Software**: Performance management software helps HR departments track and evaluate employee performance. It typically includes features such as goal setting, performance reviews, feedback collection, and performance analytics.
- **Learning Management System (LMS)**: LMS is a software that helps HR departments manage employee training and development. It allows them to create and deliver online courses, track employee progress, and manage certifications and compliance.
- **Employee Engagement Tools**: Employee engagement tools help HR departments measure and improve employee engagement and satisfaction. These tools often include employee surveys, pulse surveys, recognition programs, and communication platforms.
- **Time and Attendance Management Software**: This type of software helps HR departments manage employee attendance and time tracking. It typically includes features such as time clock integration, time-off management, and reporting capabilities.
- **HR Analytics Tools**: HR analytics tools help HR departments analyze and interpret HR data to make data-driven decisions. These tools often include dashboards, reporting capabilities, and predictive analytics.

These are just a few examples of the HR software and tools that I am familiar with. I am always eager to learn and adapt to new technologies and tools that can help in HR management.

Can you describe your experience in handling employee relations?

Answer

I have extensive experience in handling employee relations in my role as a Human Resources Manager. Some of the key aspects of my experience include:

- Developing and implementing policies and procedures related to employee relations, such as grievance handling, disciplinary actions, and conflict resolution.
- Conducting investigations into employee complaints and allegations, ensuring fairness and compliance with company policies and legal requirements.
- Providing guidance and support to managers and supervisors in dealing with employee relations issues, including coaching on effective communication and conflict resolution strategies.
- Mediating disputes between employees or between employees and management, working towards a resolution that is satisfactory for all parties involved.
- Collaborating with legal counsel and other stakeholders to ensure that employee relations practices are aligned with labor laws and regulations.
- Developing and delivering training programs on employee relations topics, such as diversity and inclusion, harassment prevention, and respectful workplace.

Throughout my career, I have successfully resolved numerous employee relations issues, fostering a positive work environment and minimizing the risk of legal disputes. I have also implemented proactive measures to enhance employee engagement and communication, such as regular feedback sessions, employee surveys, and open-door policies. By maintaining open lines of communication and promoting fairness, respect, and inclusivity, I have been able to build strong relationships with employees at all levels of the organization.

Recruitment and Talent Acquisition

Answer

Recruitment is the process of finding and hiring qualified candidates for a job opening.

Talent acquisition is a broader term that refers to the strategic approach of attracting, sourcing, and hiring top talent to meet the organization's long-term goals.

Recruitment and talent acquisition are closely related and often used interchangeably.

Recruitment and talent acquisition involve several essential steps:

- **Identifying the hiring needs**: This involves analyzing the organization's goals and workforce requirements to determine the specific skills and qualifications needed in a candidate.
- **Sourcing candidates**: This includes various methods such as job postings, referrals, social media, and professional networking to attract potential candidates.
- **Screening and selecting candidates**: This step involves reviewing resumes, conducting interviews, and assessing candidates' skills and qualifications to determine their fit for the job.
- **Making job offers**: Once a suitable candidate is identified, a job offer is made, including details on salary, benefits, and other terms of employment.
- **Onboarding**: After the candidate accepts the job offer, the onboarding process begins, which includes introducing the new employee to the organization's culture, policies, and procedures.

Real-world examples of recruitment and talent acquisition strategies include:

- Online job postings on job boards and company websites
- Employee referral programs that encourage current employees to recommend qualified candidates
- Social media recruiting, such as using LinkedIn or Facebook to connect with potential candidates
- Campus recruitment events where companies visit colleges and universities to identify and hire talented graduates
- Talent pipelines, which involve building relationships with potential candidates over time to ensure a steady supply of qualified talent when needed

In summary, recruitment and talent acquisition are essential processes for finding and hiring qualified candidates. These processes involve identifying hiring needs, sourcing candidates, screening and selecting candidates, making job offers, and onboarding new employees. Real-world strategies include online job postings, employee referral programs, social media recruiting, campus recruitment events, and talent pipelines.

How do you approach the recruitment process to attract top talent?

Answer

Develop a clear job description and candidate profile to attract the right talent.

Utilize multiple channels for job postings and advertisements, such as online job boards, social media platforms, and industry-specific websites.

Leverage employee referrals and incentivize current employees to recommend qualified candidates.

Engage in proactive sourcing techniques, such as attending industry events, networking, and reaching out to passive candidates.

Ensure a smooth and efficient application process, with clear instructions and user-friendly online forms.

Conduct thorough interviews, including behavioral-based questions and skills assessments, to assess candidate qualifications and cultural fit.

Communicate regularly with candidates throughout the process, providing updates and feedback.

Make timely and competitive job offers to top candidates, highlighting the benefits and growth opportunities within the organization.

Develop and maintain a strong employer brand, showcasing the company's values, culture, and opportunities for career advancement.

Continuously evaluate and improve the recruitment process, seeking feedback from hiring managers and candidates to identify areas for enhancement.

Can you discuss your experience with diversity and inclusion in hiring?

Answer

In my role as a Human Resources Manager, I have gained extensive experience in promoting diversity and inclusion in the hiring process. Here are some key aspects of my experience:

Implemented strategies to attract and hire candidates from diverse backgrounds, including various ethnicities, genders, and abilities.

Developed job descriptions and interview questions that focus on assessing candidates' ability to work in diverse teams and contribute to an inclusive work environment.

Partnered with diversity organizations and attended job fairs specifically targeting underrepresented groups to actively recruit diverse talent.

Established diversity metrics and tracking systems to monitor the progress of diversity and inclusion initiatives in the recruitment process.

Conducted unconscious bias training for hiring managers to ensure fair and objective evaluation of candidates.

Reviewed and updated hiring policies and procedures to eliminate any potential biases or barriers that could hinder diverse candidates from being considered.

Collaborated with management and employees to create employee resource groups and affinity networks to support and foster inclusivity in the workplace.

Regularly reported to senior leadership on the progress and outcomes of diversity and inclusion efforts in the hiring process.

Real-world examples of my experience include successfully increasing the representation of women in leadership positions by 30% within a year and hiring employees with disabilities who have made significant contributions to our organization.

Overall, my experience with diversity and inclusion in hiring has been focused on creating a fair and equitable recruitment process that values and embraces individuals from all backgrounds and perspectives.

What strategies do you use to source candidates?

Answer
- **Job Boards**: Posting job openings on popular job boards such as Indeed, LinkedIn, and Glassdoor to attract a wide pool of candidates.
- **Employee Referrals**: Encouraging current employees to refer qualified candidates for open positions. This can be done through referral bonuses or recognition programs.
- **Networking**: Attending industry events, conferences, and meetups to connect with potential candidates. Building relationships with professionals in the field can lead to referrals and recommendations.
- **Social Media**: Leveraging social media platforms like Facebook, Twitter, and Instagram to promote job openings and engage with potential candidates. Creating targeted ads and sharing content about company culture can help attract the right talent.
- **Recruitment Agencies**: Partnering with recruitment agencies or headhunters who specialize in finding qualified candidates for specific roles. These agencies have access to a large network of professionals and can help streamline the hiring process.
- **Internal Talent Pool**: Actively promoting internal job postings and considering current employees for open positions. This allows for career growth opportunities and boosts employee morale.

- **University and College Partnerships**: Building relationships with educational institutions to tap into the pool of fresh graduates. Attending career fairs, hosting information sessions, and offering internships can help identify promising candidates.
- **Online Platforms and Communities**: Engaging with online platforms and communities relevant to the industry to connect with potential candidates. This can include industry-specific forums, online job boards, and professional networking platforms like LinkedIn.
- **Passive Candidate Sourcing**: Proactively seeking out and engaging with passive candidates who may not be actively looking for a job but possess the skills and experience desired. This can be done through targeted outreach, networking, and building relationships.
- **Talent Pipelining**: Building and maintaining a talent pipeline of potential candidates for future positions. This involves consistently sourcing, engaging, and nurturing relationships with potential candidates, even if there are no immediate job openings.

How do you ensure a positive candidate experience?

Answer

- Provide clear and detailed job descriptions and requirements to set proper expectations for candidates.
- Be responsive and timely in communication with candidates, keeping them informed about the status of their application.
- Offer a streamlined and user-friendly application process, minimizing unnecessary steps and eliminating technical issues.
- Ensure a welcoming and professional interview experience, making candidates feel comfortable and valued.
- Provide feedback to candidates after interviews, even if they were not selected, to show respect for their time and effort.
- Personalize the candidate experience by addressing individual concerns and needs.
- Maintain transparency throughout the hiring process, sharing information about the company culture, team dynamics, and growth opportunities.
- Collect and act on candidate feedback to continuously improve the recruitment process.
- Follow up with candidates promptly, whether they are selected or not, to provide closure and maintain a positive impression of the company.
- Treat candidates with respect and empathy, ensuring a fair and unbiased evaluation.
- Create a seamless onboarding process for selected candidates, helping them transition smoothly into the company.
- Provide a positive candidate experience can enhance the employer brand and attract top talent.

Employee Relations

Answer

Employee relations is a crucial aspect of human resources management that focuses on maintaining positive and productive relationships between employers and employees.

Key objectives of employee relations include creating a harmonious work environment, promoting employee engagement and satisfaction, managing conflicts and grievances, and ensuring compliance with labor laws and regulations.

In order to effectively manage employee relations, human resources managers need to have a good understanding of the needs and expectations of both employees and employers. They also need to be skilled in communication, conflict resolution, and negotiation.

Real-world examples of employee relations activities include:

- Implementing employee engagement initiatives such as recognition programs and team-building activities to improve morale and job satisfaction.
- Resolving conflicts between employees or between employees and management through mediation or other conflict resolution techniques.
- Investigating and addressing employee grievances, such as complaints about workplace harassment or unfair treatment.
- Developing and implementing policies and procedures that ensure compliance with labor laws and regulations, such as those related to minimum wage, working hours, and employee benefits.
- Providing training and development opportunities to enhance employees' skills and job performance.
- Conducting employee opinion surveys to gather feedback and identify areas for improvement.
- Developing and maintaining effective channels of communication between employees and management, such as regular team meetings or employee newsletters.
- Handling disciplinary actions, such as issuing warnings or implementing performance improvement plans.
- Managing employee terminations and conducting exit interviews to understand reasons for leaving and identify potential areas for improvement.
- Supporting employee well-being and work-life balance initiatives, such as flexible work arrangements or employee assistance programs.

Describe a challenging employee relations issue you've resolved.

Answer

I once encountered a challenging employee relations issue where two employees in my team had a serious conflict that was affecting the overall morale and productivity of the team.

To resolve the issue, I took the following steps:

- **Gathered information**: I first met with both employees separately to understand their perspectives and gather information about the situation. I listened actively and asked probing questions to get a complete picture of the issue.
- **Identified the root cause**: Based on the information gathered, I identified the root cause of the conflict, which was a misunderstanding and miscommunication about the division of work and responsibilities.
- **Facilitated a meeting**: I organized a meeting with both employees to address the issue. I created a safe and neutral space for them to express their concerns and feelings. I encouraged open and honest communication, ensuring that both parties had an equal opportunity to speak.
- **Mediated the discussion**: During the meeting, I acted as a mediator, ensuring that the conversation remained respectful and focused on finding a resolution. I facilitated a constructive dialogue between the two employees, helping them understand each other's perspectives and find common ground.
- **Developed an action plan**: Once the employees had reached a mutual understanding, I worked with them to develop an action plan to prevent similar conflicts in the future. This included clearly defining roles and responsibilities, improving communication channels, and setting up regular check-ins to address any concerns before they escalate.
- **Followed up**: After the resolution of the conflict, I followed up with both employees individually to ensure that the issue was fully resolved and that they felt supported. I also monitored the team dynamics closely in the following weeks to ensure that no further issues arose.

This approach helped in resolving the employee relations issue effectively, restoring a positive work environment and improving team collaboration and productivity.

Real-world example: In a previous role as a Human Resources Manager, I dealt with a situation where two team members were constantly arguing and blaming each other for mistakes. This had a significant impact on their work as well as the overall team dynamics. By following the steps mentioned above, I was able to mediate the conflict and help the employees understand each other's perspectives. They were able to work together more effectively and the team's performance improved as a result.

How do you handle conflicts between employees or teams?

Answer

As a Human Resources Manager, my role is to help resolve conflicts between employees or teams in a fair and constructive manner. Here are the steps I would take to handle conflicts:

- **Gather information**: I would first gather information about the conflict by speaking to the involved parties, reviewing any relevant documents or emails, and talking to witnesses if necessary. This would help me understand the root cause of the conflict and the different perspectives involved.

- **Listen to all parties**: I would provide a safe and confidential space for all parties to express their concerns and feelings. It is important to actively listen to each person involved and ensure that they feel heard and understood.
- **Mediate a discussion**: I would facilitate a discussion between the conflicting parties, encouraging open communication and respectful dialogues. This would involve setting ground rules for the discussion, allowing each person to speak without interruption, and guiding the conversation towards finding a resolution.
- **Identify common interests**: I would work with the parties to identify any common interests or goals that they share. By focusing on shared objectives, it becomes easier to find common ground and reach a mutually acceptable solution.
- **Explore possible solutions**: I would encourage the parties to brainstorm possible solutions to the conflict. This could involve suggesting compromises, alternative approaches, or seeking advice from supervisors or other team members.
- **Reach a resolution**: Once the parties have explored different solutions, I would help them evaluate the pros and cons of each option and guide them towards reaching a resolution. This could involve negotiating a compromise or implementing a decision that is fair and reasonable for all parties involved.
- **Follow-up and monitor**: After the conflict has been resolved, I would follow up with the parties involved to ensure that the resolution is being implemented effectively. I would also monitor the situation to prevent any potential reoccurrence of the conflict and provide any necessary support or coaching.

By following these steps, I aim to resolve conflicts in a fair and constructive manner, fostering a positive work environment and maintaining good relationships between employees and teams.

What steps do you take to foster a positive work environment?

Answer
- Clearly communicate expectations and goals to employees, ensuring they understand their roles and responsibilities.
- Encourage open and transparent communication among team members, allowing for feedback, suggestions, and concerns to be shared.
- Recognize and appreciate employees' efforts and achievements, providing positive reinforcement and rewards.
- Promote work-life balance by offering flexible schedules, remote work options, and wellness programs.
- Provide opportunities for growth and development through training programs, mentoring, and career advancement opportunities.
- Foster a sense of teamwork and collaboration by promoting cross-functional projects and team-building activities.
- Create a safe and inclusive work environment, where diversity is valued and everyone feels respected and supported.

- Implement policies and procedures that promote fairness and equality, such as unbiased hiring practices and performance evaluations.
- Lead by example and cultivate a positive company culture, demonstrating integrity, empathy, and professionalism.
- Regularly gather feedback from employees through surveys, focus groups, or one-on-one meetings to understand their needs and address any issues.

How do you address employee grievances?

Answer

- Listen to the employee: As a Human Resources Manager, it is important to provide a safe and comfortable space for employees to voice their concerns. When an employee comes forward with a grievance, it is crucial to actively listen to their perspective and understand the issue at hand.
- Investigate the grievance: Once the grievance has been brought to your attention, it is your responsibility to conduct a thorough investigation. This may involve gathering relevant information, interviewing involved parties, and reviewing any applicable policies or procedures.
- Maintain confidentiality: It is essential to maintain strict confidentiality throughout the grievance process. This includes not discussing the details of the grievance with individuals who are not directly involved in the resolution process.
- Take appropriate action: Based on the findings of the investigation, you should take appropriate action to address the grievance. This may involve implementing disciplinary measures, providing additional training or support, or making changes to policies or procedures to prevent similar issues from arising in the future.
- Communicate the outcome: Once a resolution has been reached, it is important to communicate the outcome to the employee who raised the grievance. This should be done in a timely and clear manner, ensuring that the employee understands the actions that have been taken and any next steps that may be necessary.
- Follow up: Following the resolution of a grievance, it is important to follow up with the employee to ensure that they are satisfied with the outcome and to address any lingering concerns or issues. This demonstrates a commitment to ongoing support and employee engagement.
- Real-world example: Let's say an employee raises a grievance about unfair treatment by a supervisor. As a Human Resources Manager, you would listen to the employee's concerns, gather relevant information, and conduct interviews with both the employee and the supervisor. After a thorough investigation, you may find that the supervisor has indeed been treating the employee unfairly. In this case, you would take appropriate action, such as implementing disciplinary measures or providing additional training to the supervisor. You would then communicate the outcome to the employee and follow up to ensure their satisfaction and address any remaining concerns.

Performance Management

Answer

Performance management is the ongoing process of setting objectives, assessing progress, and providing feedback and support to employees to ensure that they are meeting their goals and contributing to the overall success of the organization.

It involves several key components:

- **Goal setting**: Managers work with employees to set clear and specific goals that align with the organization's objectives. These goals should be measurable and achievable.
- **Performance monitoring**: Managers regularly track and monitor employees' progress towards their goals. This can be done through regular check-ins, progress reports, or performance reviews.
- **Feedback and coaching**: Managers provide timely and constructive feedback to employees on their performance. They also offer guidance and support to help employees improve and develop their skills.
- **Recognition and rewards**: Performance management includes recognizing and rewarding employees who consistently meet or exceed their goals. This can be in the form of bonuses, promotions, or other incentives.

Real-world example: In a sales team, performance management may involve setting sales targets for each team member, monitoring their progress through regular sales reports, providing feedback on their sales techniques, and rewarding top performers with bonuses.

Performance management is important for several reasons:

- It helps align individual and team goals with organizational objectives, ensuring that everyone is working towards the same goals.
- It provides clarity and direction to employees, helping them understand what is expected of them and how their work contributes to the overall success of the organization.
- It promotes continuous improvement and development, as employees receive feedback and coaching to help them grow and enhance their skills.
- It enables the identification of high performers and supports the retention of top talent through recognition and rewards.

Overall, performance management is a critical function of a Human Resources Manager, as it helps drive employee engagement, productivity, and organizational success.

Explain your approach to performance reviews.

Answer

Performance reviews are an essential tool for evaluating and improving employee performance. My approach to performance reviews is focused on providing constructive feedback, setting clear goals, and promoting growth and development.

I believe in a collaborative approach where both the manager and the employee are actively involved in the review process. This ensures that both parties have a chance to share their perspectives and work together to identify areas of improvement and set realistic goals for the future.

To ensure clarity and simplicity in the performance review process, I follow these steps:

- **Preparation**: Before the review, I gather relevant data and information, such as performance metrics, feedback from colleagues, and examples of both strengths and areas for improvement.
- **Setting the Stage**: At the beginning of the performance review meeting, I set a positive and open tone, emphasizing the purpose of the review and the importance of constructive feedback in personal and professional growth.
- **Feedback**: I provide specific, actionable, and timely feedback on the employee's performance, highlighting both their accomplishments and areas for improvement. I use real-world examples and specific data to support my feedback and ensure clarity.
- **Goal Setting**: Together with the employee, I set clear and achievable goals for the future. These goals are aligned with the overall objectives of the organization and take into account the employee's strengths and development areas.
- **Development Plan**: I work with the employee to create a personalized development plan that includes specific steps and resources needed to achieve their goals. This plan may include training opportunities, mentoring, or additional responsibilities.
- **Follow-up**: I schedule regular check-ins to monitor progress, provide ongoing feedback, and make any necessary adjustments to the development plan. This ensures that the goals are being met and that the employee feels supported and valued.

Overall, my approach to performance reviews is aimed at creating a positive and constructive environment where employees can grow, develop, and contribute to the success of the organization.

How do you handle underperforming employees?

Answer

- **Identify the underperformance**: The first step is to clearly identify the underperforming employee and the specific areas where they are falling short. This can be done through performance evaluations, feedback from coworkers or customers, or monitoring their work closely.

- **Communicate expectations**: Once the underperformance has been identified, it is important to communicate clear expectations to the employee. This includes outlining the specific areas where improvement is needed, setting goals and deadlines, and explaining the consequences of continued underperformance.
- **Provide support and resources**: In some cases, underperformance may be due to a lack of skills or knowledge. As a manager, it is important to provide the necessary support and resources to help the employee improve. This could include additional training, mentoring, or coaching.
- **Offer feedback and guidance**: Regular feedback and guidance are essential in helping underperforming employees improve. This can be done through one-on-one meetings, performance reviews, or ongoing check-ins. It is important to provide constructive feedback, highlighting both the areas where improvement is needed and the employee's strengths.
- **Set clear consequences**: While providing support and guidance, it is also important to set clear consequences for continued underperformance. This could include verbal warnings, written warnings, or ultimately, termination of employment. It is important to follow any company policies or procedures when implementing consequences.
- **Document performance**: Throughout the process of addressing underperformance, it is crucial to document everything. This includes performance evaluations, feedback, and any disciplinary actions taken. This documentation can be useful in tracking progress, justifying decisions, and protecting the company legally.
- **Monitor progress and adjust strategies**: As the employee works on improving their performance, it is important to regularly monitor their progress. This can be done through ongoing feedback, performance evaluations, or objective metrics. If the initial strategies are not working, it may be necessary to adjust and try different approaches to help the employee succeed.
- **Recognize and reward improvement**: When an underperforming employee shows improvement, it is important to recognize and reward their efforts. This can be done through verbal praise, incentives, or opportunities for growth and development. Recognizing and rewarding improvement can help motivate the employee to continue striving for excellence.

Can you share a successful performance improvement plan you implemented?

Answer

Yes, I can share a successful performance improvement plan that I implemented as a Human Resources Manager. The plan was implemented for an employee who was consistently missing project deadlines and not meeting productivity targets.

The steps of the performance improvement plan were as follows:

- **Clearly defined expectations and goals**: I met with the employee to discuss their job responsibilities, performance expectations, and set specific goals for improvement.

- **Regular feedback and coaching**: I provided ongoing feedback and coaching to the employee, offering guidance on how to improve their time management skills and productivity.
- **Training and development**: I identified areas where the employee needed additional training or development and provided resources to help them enhance their skills.
- **Performance monitoring**: I implemented a system to track the employee's progress and provided regular updates on their performance to ensure they were aware of their improvement areas.
- **Performance review and recognition**: After a set period of time, I conducted a performance review with the employee to evaluate their progress and provide recognition for their improvements.

The performance improvement plan was successful, as the employee showed significant improvement in meeting project deadlines and increasing productivity.

What metrics do you use to measure employee performance?

Answer

There are several metrics that can be used to measure employee performance:

- **Key Performance Indicators (KPIs)**: These are specific goals and targets that are set for each employee. They can be quantitative or qualitative and are used to track progress and measure performance against expectations.
- **Productivity**: This metric measures the amount of work completed by an employee within a given time period. It can be measured in terms of output, sales, or other relevant factors.
- **Quality of Work**: This metric assesses the accuracy, attention to detail, and overall quality of the work produced by an employee.
- **Attendance and Punctuality**: This metric measures the frequency and timeliness of an employee's attendance at work.
- **Customer Satisfaction**: This metric measures the level of satisfaction or dissatisfaction of customers with the service or product provided by an employee.
- **Team Collaboration**: This metric assesses the ability of an employee to work effectively and collaborate with team members.

Real-world examples of these metrics include:

- For KPIs, an example could be a sales target that an employee needs to meet.
- Productivity can be measured by the number of units produced by a factory worker in a day.
- Quality of work can be assessed through customer feedback or through a review process.
- Attendance and punctuality can be measured by tracking the number of times an employee arrives late or takes unscheduled absences.
- Customer satisfaction can be measured through surveys or feedback forms.

- Team collaboration can be assessed through peer evaluations or feedback from team members.

In summary, the metrics used to measure employee performance can vary depending on the nature of the job and the organization's goals. However, common metrics include KPIs, productivity, quality of work, attendance and punctuality, customer satisfaction, and team collaboration.

Training and Development

Answer

Training and development is an essential aspect of the role of a Human Resources Manager. It involves providing employees with the necessary skills and knowledge to perform their job effectively and to further their professional growth. Here are some key points about training and development:

- Training programs can be designed to address specific needs and gaps in employee skills. For example, if there is a need for improved customer service skills, a training program can be developed to focus on that area.
- Development programs, on the other hand, are more focused on preparing employees for future roles and responsibilities. These programs can include activities such as job rotations, mentoring, and coaching.
- Training and development can take various forms, including classroom training, on-the-job training, workshops, e-learning, and conferences. The choice of method depends on the nature of the skills being developed and the preferences of the employees.
- Real-world examples of training and development initiatives include leadership development programs, technical skill training, and diversity and inclusion training.
- It is important for Human Resources Managers to regularly assess the effectiveness of training and development programs. This can be done through evaluations, feedback from employees and managers, and monitoring performance improvement.
- Training and development programs should have clear objectives and outcomes. This helps in measuring the success of the programs and aligning them with organizational goals.

How do you assess training needs within an organization?

Answer

- Conduct a training needs assessment (TNA) to identify the skill gaps and areas where training is required.
- Collect data through surveys, interviews, and focus groups to understand the current knowledge, skills, and performance levels of employees.
- Analyze job descriptions and performance evaluations to identify the specific competencies and skills required for each role.
- Observe employees in their work environment to identify areas where they may be struggling or lacking skills.
- Review feedback from supervisors and managers to understand the training needs and areas of improvement.
- Consider the organization's strategic goals and objectives to align training needs with the overall business objectives.
- Use technology-based tools, such as learning management systems, to track employee performance and identify areas for improvement.
- Prioritize training needs based on urgency, impact on business performance, and feasibility of training interventions.

- Develop a comprehensive training plan that includes objectives, content, delivery methods, and evaluation criteria.
- Regularly review and update the training needs assessment process to ensure it remains relevant and effective.

Can you describe a successful employee development program you've implemented?

Answer

Yes, I can describe a successful employee development program that I have implemented.

In my previous role as a Human Resources Manager, I implemented a comprehensive employee development program that had a positive impact on the organization.

Here are the key components and strategies of the program:

- **Needs Assessment**: We conducted a thorough assessment of the skills and competencies required by employees at different levels within the organization.
- **Individual Development Plans (IDPs)**: Based on the needs assessment, we worked with each employee to create personalized IDPs that outlined their developmental goals and identified specific actions and resources needed to achieve those goals.
- **Training and Development Opportunities**: We provided a range of training and development opportunities, including workshops, seminars, online courses, and mentoring programs.
- **Performance Feedback and Coaching**: We implemented a performance feedback system that included regular check-ins, goal-setting, and coaching sessions to support employees in their development.
- **Talent Mobility**: We encouraged employees to explore different roles and departments within the organization to gain new experiences and expand their skill set.
- **Recognition and Rewards**: We recognized and rewarded employees who actively participated in the employee development program and achieved their developmental goals.
- **Evaluation and Continuous Improvement**: We regularly evaluated the effectiveness of the program through feedback surveys, performance reviews, and metrics such as employee engagement and retention rates. Based on the feedback received, we made necessary adjustments and improvements to the program.

As a result of this employee development program, we observed the following benefits:

- Increased employee engagement and motivation
- Improved employee performance and productivity
- Enhanced employee satisfaction and retention
- Development of a skilled and adaptable workforce
- Succession planning and talent pipeline development

How do you measure the effectiveness of training initiatives?

Answer

One way to measure the effectiveness of training initiatives is to conduct pre- and post-training assessments to compare the knowledge and skills gained by employees.

Another method is to track the performance of employees before and after the training to see if there is an improvement in their job performance.

Feedback from employees can also be valuable in measuring the effectiveness of training initiatives. Surveys or interviews can be conducted to gather their opinions and experiences.

Additionally, the retention rate of the training material can be measured by assessing how well employees remember and apply what they have learned over time.

Return on investment (ROI) can also be used as a measure of training effectiveness. This involves comparing the cost of the training program to the benefits it brings to the organization, such as increased productivity or reduced turnover.

Real-world examples of measuring training effectiveness could include:

- A company implementing a customer service training program could track customer satisfaction ratings before and after the training to see if there is an improvement.
- An organization conducting leadership development training could measure the number of employees who are promoted or take on additional responsibilities after completing the program.
- A manufacturing company could measure the reduction in accidents or errors on the production line after implementing safety training.

Summarized Answer:

The effectiveness of training initiatives can be measured through pre- and post-training assessments, tracking employee performance, gathering feedback from employees, assessing retention of training material, and calculating the return on investment. Real-world examples include tracking customer satisfaction ratings, measuring employee promotions or increased responsibilities, and assessing the reduction in accidents or errors.

How do you encourage ongoing learning among employees?

Answer
- Provide regular training sessions and workshops on topics relevant to their roles and professional development.

- Offer opportunities for employees to attend conferences, webinars, and industry events to learn from experts and network with peers.
- Create a culture of continuous learning by emphasizing the importance of ongoing education and development.
- Recognize and reward employees who actively seek out learning opportunities and share their knowledge with others.
- Establish mentorship programs where experienced employees can guide and support less experienced colleagues.
- Encourage employees to set personal development goals and provide resources and support to help them achieve those goals.
- Utilize technology and e-learning platforms to provide accessible and flexible learning options.
- Promote knowledge sharing within the organization through platforms like intranets, forums, and collaborative tools.
- Provide opportunities for employees to apply their learning in real-world scenarios through projects and assignments.
- Regularly assess and evaluate the effectiveness of learning initiatives to make improvements and ensure they align with organizational goals.

HR Policies and Compliance

Answer

HR policies are a set of rules and guidelines that are developed by an organization to govern the behavior and actions of its employees.

Compliance refers to the act of adhering to these policies and ensuring that employees follow them.

HR policies and compliance are crucial for maintaining a fair and productive work environment.

They help in setting expectations, providing guidance, and ensuring consistency in decision-making.

Some common HR policies include:

- **Code of conduct**: This policy outlines the expected behavior and ethics of employees.
- **Anti-discrimination and harassment policy**: This policy ensures that employees are treated fairly and without any form of discrimination or harassment.
- **Leave policy**: This policy defines the rules and procedures for taking different types of leaves, such as sick leave, vacation leave, and maternity/paternity leave.
- **Performance management policy**: This policy establishes the criteria and processes for evaluating employee performance and providing feedback.
- **Confidentiality policy**: This policy specifies how employees should handle and protect confidential and sensitive information.

Compliance with HR policies is essential for avoiding legal issues and maintaining a positive work culture.

For example, if an organization fails to comply with anti-discrimination policies, it may face lawsuits and damage to its reputation.

To ensure compliance, organizations may implement various measures such as:

- **Regular training sessions**: These sessions educate employees about HR policies and the importance of compliance.
- **Policy acknowledgment**: Employees are required to sign an acknowledgment form stating that they have read and understood the HR policies.
- **Monitoring and enforcement**: HR managers monitor employee behavior and take appropriate action if policies are violated.

In summary, HR policies and compliance play a crucial role in maintaining a fair and productive work environment. They provide guidelines for employee behavior and help in avoiding legal issues.

Organizations should regularly review and update their policies to adapt to changing laws and business needs.

How do you ensure company policies are communicated and followed?

Answer

- Create a clear and concise policy handbook that outlines all company policies and procedures.
- Distribute the policy handbook to all employees and ensure they have access to it at all times.
- Hold regular meetings or training sessions to review company policies and answer any questions employees may have.
- Use different communication channels such as email, intranet, or bulletin boards to remind employees of important policies and any updates or changes.
- Provide real-world examples and case studies to illustrate the importance of following company policies.
- Implement a system to track and monitor policy compliance, such as an employee self-reporting tool or regular audits.
- Encourage open communication and feedback from employees to address any concerns or issues related to company policies.
- Recognize and reward employees who consistently demonstrate adherence to company policies.
- Take appropriate disciplinary actions for policy violations to ensure accountability and maintain a culture of compliance.

Can you discuss your experience with labor laws and compliance?

Answer

I have extensive experience with labor laws and compliance as a Human Resources Manager. Some key points about my experience include:

- **Familiarity with federal and state labor laws**: I have a deep understanding of the Fair Labor Standards Act (FLSA), the Family and Medical Leave Act (FMLA), and the Americans with Disabilities Act (ADA), among others. I stay up-to-date with the latest changes in these laws to ensure our company remains in compliance.
- **Conducting regular audits**: I regularly conduct audits to ensure that our company is following all labor laws and regulations. This involves reviewing our policies and procedures, identifying any areas of non-compliance, and implementing corrective measures.
- **Training and education**: I have developed and delivered training programs for employees and managers to ensure they understand their rights and responsibilities under labor laws. This includes topics such as proper classification of employees, overtime rules, and anti-discrimination laws.
- **Handling complaints and investigations**: I have experience investigating and resolving complaints related to labor law violations. This includes conducting interviews, gathering evidence, and taking appropriate action to address any violations.

- **Collaborating with legal counsel**: I work closely with our legal counsel to ensure that our company remains compliant with labor laws. This includes seeking advice on complex issues, reviewing policies and procedures, and staying informed about any legal developments that may impact our operations.
- **Engaging with regulatory agencies**: I have experience interacting with government agencies such as the Equal Employment Opportunity Commission (EEOC) and the Department of Labor (DOL). This includes responding to inquiries, providing requested documentation, and participating in any audits or investigations.

Overall, my experience with labor laws and compliance is comprehensive and up-to-date. I am dedicated to ensuring that our company operates ethically and in accordance with all applicable laws and regulations.

How do you handle HR issues in multiple locations or countries?

Answer
- Establish a centralized HR department that oversees all locations or countries.
- Create clear and consistent HR policies and procedures that apply to all locations or countries.
- Ensure that the HR team has a good understanding of the laws and regulations in each location or country.
- Implement technology solutions that facilitate communication and collaboration between HR and employees in different locations or countries.
- Develop a global HR strategy that takes into account the unique cultural and legal differences of each location or country.
- Regularly review and update HR policies and procedures to adapt to changes in laws or regulations.
- Provide training and development opportunities for HR professionals to enhance their knowledge and skills in managing HR issues in multiple locations or countries.
- Establish strong relationships with local HR professionals or consultants in each location or country to gain insights into local practices and regulations.
- Create a system for tracking and reporting HR metrics and performance indicators to ensure consistency and accountability across locations or countries.

What steps do you take to maintain confidentiality in HR matters?

Answer
- Implement strict confidentiality policies and procedures that outline the importance of maintaining confidentiality in HR matters. These policies should include guidelines on who has access to sensitive information, how it should be stored and shared, and the consequences of violating confidentiality.

- Provide regular training to all HR staff on the importance of confidentiality and the specific procedures they need to follow to maintain it. This training should cover topics such as handling sensitive employee data, maintaining the confidentiality of investigations and disciplinary actions, and the proper use of HR systems and tools.

- Limit access to sensitive HR information by implementing security measures such as password protection, encryption, and role-based access controls. Only authorized personnel should have access to sensitive data, and they should be required to follow strict protocols for accessing and handling it.

- Use secure systems and technologies to store and transmit HR data. This can include secure file servers, encrypted email and messaging platforms, and secure cloud storage solutions.

- Regularly review and update confidentiality policies and procedures to ensure they align with current best practices and legal requirements. This can include conducting privacy impact assessments, implementing data protection measures, and staying up to date with relevant laws and regulations.

- Monitor and audit HR processes and systems to detect and prevent unauthorized access or disclosure of sensitive information. This can involve regular security audits, access logs, and incident response procedures.

- Foster a culture of confidentiality and trust within the HR department. This can be done by promoting the importance of confidentiality, leading by example, and creating an environment where employees feel comfortable reporting any breaches or concerns about confidentiality.

Strategic HR Planning

Answer

Strategic HR planning is the process of aligning the human resources function with the overall strategic goals and objectives of an organization.

It involves identifying the workforce requirements needed to achieve these goals and developing strategies to attract, retain, and develop the necessary talent.

Strategic HR planning is crucial for organizations as it ensures that they have the right people in the right positions at the right time.

This includes forecasting future talent needs, analyzing the current workforce, and identifying gaps in skills or competencies.

Real-world examples of strategic HR planning include:

- A company that is expanding its operations globally and needs to plan for the recruitment and development of employees in different countries and cultures.
- A company that is undergoing a digital transformation and needs to identify the skills and capabilities required for the new technology-driven roles.
- A company that is facing an aging workforce and needs to develop succession plans to ensure a smooth transition of knowledge and skills.

To summarize, strategic HR planning involves aligning the HR function with the organization's strategic goals, forecasting future talent needs, analyzing the current workforce, and developing strategies to attract, retain, and develop the necessary talent.

How do you align HR strategies with overall business goals?

Answer

Understand the business goals: The first step to align HR strategies with overall business goals is to have a clear understanding of the organization's objectives and priorities.

Identify HR priorities: Once the business goals are understood, HR needs to identify the key areas where they can contribute to achieving those goals. This could include talent acquisition, talent development, performance management, or employee engagement.

Develop HR strategies: Once the HR priorities are identified, HR strategies need to be developed to address those priorities. These strategies should be aligned with the business goals and take into account the organization's culture, resources, and capabilities.

Example: If the business goal is to expand into new markets, HR can develop a talent acquisition strategy to attract and hire employees with the necessary skills and experience in those markets.

Implement HR initiatives: Once the HR strategies are developed, they need to be implemented through various HR initiatives and programs. These initiatives could include recruitment and selection processes, training and development programs, performance management systems, or employee engagement activities.

Monitor and evaluate: It is important to continuously monitor and evaluate the effectiveness of HR initiatives in contributing to the achievement of business goals. This can be done through regular feedback from managers and employees, data analysis, and metrics.

Make necessary adjustments: Based on the monitoring and evaluation, necessary adjustments should be made to HR strategies and initiatives to ensure they remain aligned with the changing business goals and needs.

Summary: Aligning HR strategies with overall business goals involves understanding the business goals, identifying HR priorities, developing HR strategies, implementing HR initiatives, monitoring and evaluating their effectiveness, and making necessary adjustments.

Can you describe your involvement in organizational restructuring or downsizing?

Answer

As a Human Resources Manager, I have been actively involved in organizational restructuring and downsizing initiatives. Here is how I have contributed:

Conducted a thorough analysis of the organization's structure and identified areas that required reorganization or downsizing.

Worked closely with top management and department heads to develop a strategic plan for restructuring or downsizing.

Developed a communication plan to ensure that employees were informed about the changes and understood the reasons behind them.

Collaborated with the legal team to ensure compliance with all relevant employment laws and regulations.

Managed the implementation of the restructuring or downsizing plan, which involved coordinating with different departments, communicating with employees, and addressing any concerns or questions.

Provided support to managers and supervisors in handling the emotional and practical aspects of the restructuring or downsizing process.

Conducted training sessions for managers and supervisors to equip them with the necessary skills to effectively manage the changes and support their teams.

Monitored the progress of the restructuring or downsizing initiatives and made necessary adjustments as required.

Ensured that all documentation related to the restructuring or downsizing was properly maintained and updated.

Summary: My involvement in organizational restructuring or downsizing has been comprehensive, from analyzing the need for change to implementing the plan and supporting managers and employees throughout the process. I have successfully navigated the legal and emotional aspects of these initiatives while ensuring compliance and effective communication.

What role do HR professionals play in strategic planning?

Answer

HR professionals play a critical role in strategic planning as they are responsible for aligning the organization's human resources with its strategic goals and objectives.

They work closely with top management to understand the organization's strategic direction and develop HR strategies that support the achievement of those goals.

HR professionals analyze the workforce needs of the organization and identify the skills and competencies required to execute the strategic plan.

They develop recruitment and selection strategies to attract and hire individuals who possess the necessary skills and competencies.

HR professionals also develop training and development programs to ensure that employees have the knowledge and skills required to contribute to the organization's strategic objectives.

They are responsible for performance management, including setting performance targets and providing feedback and coaching to employees to help them meet those targets.

HR professionals also play a role in succession planning, ensuring that the organization has a pipeline of talent to fill key roles as needed.

They monitor and evaluate the effectiveness of HR strategies and make adjustments as necessary to ensure alignment with the strategic plan.

HR professionals also provide guidance and support to managers and employees in implementing the strategic plan, including communicating the plan, monitoring progress, and addressing any barriers or challenges that arise.

How do you anticipate and address future HR challenges?

Answer

Stay updated on industry trends and changes

Utilize data and analytics to make informed decisions

Develop a flexible and adaptable workforce

Invest in employee training and development

Build a strong employer brand

Embrace technology and automation

Foster a culture of continuous learning and improvement

Collaborate with other HR professionals and industry experts .

Summary

Leadership and Collaboration

Answer

Leadership and collaboration are crucial skills for a Human Resources Manager. Here are some key points to consider:

- Leadership involves guiding and motivating a team to achieve common goals. As a Human Resources Manager, you will be responsible for leading your HR team and working with other departments within the organization. This requires strong communication, decision-making, and problem-solving skills.
- Collaboration involves working effectively with others to achieve a shared objective. As a Human Resources Manager, you will need to collaborate with employees at all levels, from entry-level staff to senior executives. This includes building relationships, facilitating teamwork, and promoting a culture of collaboration within the organization.
- **Real-world example**: Let's say your organization is going through a major organizational change, such as a merger or acquisition. As a Human Resources Manager, you would need to demonstrate leadership by providing clear direction and guidance to your HR team during this transition. You would also need to collaborate with other departments, such as finance and operations, to ensure a smooth integration of HR processes and policies.
- **Hands-on exercise**: Take a scenario where there is a conflict between two employees in your organization. As a Human Resources Manager, demonstrate your leadership skills by addressing the conflict in a fair and effective manner. Collaborate with the employees involved, listen to their perspectives, and find a resolution that benefits both parties.
- **Visual aids**: Use a diagram to illustrate the different levels of leadership within an organization and how collaboration flows between departments. This can help visually represent the importance of leadership and collaboration in the HR Manager role.
- **Engaging formatting**: Use headings, subheadings, and bullet points to break down information and make it easier to read and understand. This helps with clarity and ensures key points are highlighted.
- **Logical progression**: Present the information in a logical order, starting with an introduction to leadership and collaboration, followed by examples and exercises to reinforce the concepts.
- **Clear objectives**: Clearly state the objectives of leadership and collaboration in the context of the HR Manager role. This helps the reader understand the purpose and importance of developing these skills.

How do you collaborate with other departments within the organization?

Answer

Establish regular communication channels: As a Human Resources Manager, it is important to establish regular communication channels with other departments within the organization. This can be done through regular meetings, email updates, or even a shared collaboration platform. By having a clear line of communication, it becomes easier to coordinate efforts and address any potential issues that may arise.

Build relationships: Building relationships with other departments is crucial for effective collaboration. By getting to know the individuals in other departments, you can better understand their needs and priorities, and find common ground for collaboration. This can be done through informal conversations, team-building activities, or even joint projects.

Collaborate on projects: Collaborating on projects is a great way to foster teamwork and cross-departmental collaboration. By involving representatives from different departments in a project, you can leverage their expertise and perspectives to create better outcomes. For example, if the HR department is working on implementing a new performance management system, involving representatives from the IT department can ensure that the system is integrated with existing IT infrastructure.

Share information and resources: Sharing information and resources is essential for effective collaboration. This can involve sharing data, reports, or even sharing physical resources such as meeting rooms or equipment. By sharing information and resources, departments can work together more efficiently and avoid duplication of effort.

Provide training and support: To promote collaboration between departments, it is important to provide training and support. This can involve providing training on collaboration tools and techniques, or even facilitating workshops or team-building activities. By equipping employees with the necessary skills and knowledge, they can collaborate more effectively with other departments.

Summary: As a Human Resources Manager, collaborating with other departments within the organization is crucial for achieving organizational goals. By establishing regular communication channels, building relationships, collaborating on projects, sharing information and resources, and providing training and support, HR managers can foster a culture of collaboration and teamwork.

Can you share an example of when you had to influence senior management?

Answer
In my role as a Human Resources Manager, I have had several instances where I needed to influence senior management to make important decisions or changes.

One example was when I proposed a new employee wellness program to senior management. The program aimed to promote healthy habits and work-life balance among employees, which could result in increased productivity and reduced healthcare costs for the company.

To influence senior management, I first conducted research on the benefits of employee wellness programs and gathered data on the potential cost savings. I then prepared a comprehensive presentation, including real-world examples of other companies that had successfully implemented similar programs.

During the presentation, I used visual aids such as charts and graphs to illustrate the potential impact on employee engagement and overall company performance. I also shared testimonials from employees who had participated in pilot programs, highlighting their positive experiences and improved well-being.

To further support my proposal, I included a detailed budget and timeline, outlining the resources required and the expected return on investment.

After the presentation, I engaged in open discussions with senior management, addressing any concerns or objections they had. I emphasized the long-term benefits of the program and how it aligned with the company's values and goals.

Through my efforts to provide clear, concise information and compelling arguments, I was able to successfully influence senior management to approve the employee wellness program.

The program was implemented company-wide, and we saw positive results in terms of improved employee morale, decreased absenteeism, and lower healthcare costs.

In summary, as a Human Resources Manager, influencing senior management is an essential part of my role. By conducting thorough research, preparing a compelling presentation, and engaging in open discussions, I have been able to successfully influence senior management to make important decisions and changes.

How do you lead and develop your HR team?

Answer

Set clear expectations and communicate effectively: As a leader, it is important to set clear expectations for your HR team and communicate them effectively. This includes defining their roles and responsibilities, as well as any specific goals or targets they need to achieve. By doing so, you provide them with a clear direction and purpose, which helps to motivate and guide their work.

Provide ongoing training and development opportunities: In order to develop your HR team, it is crucial to provide them with ongoing training and development opportunities. This can include attending workshops, conferences, or webinars related to HR practices and trends. Additionally, you can encourage your team members to pursue certifications or further education in HR. By investing in their professional growth, you not only enhance their skills and knowledge but also show that you value their development.

Encourage collaboration and teamwork: Building a strong HR team requires fostering a collaborative and supportive environment. Encourage your team members to work together, share knowledge, and support one another. This can be done through regular team meetings, brainstorming sessions, or group projects. By promoting collaboration, you can leverage the diverse skills and experiences of your team members, resulting in more effective problem-solving and decision-making.

Recognize and reward achievements: It is important to recognize and reward the achievements of your HR team members. This can be done through verbal praise, written acknowledgments, or even small incentives or bonuses. By acknowledging their hard work and contributions, you not only boost their morale but also reinforce positive behaviors and motivate them to continue performing at a high level.

Provide feedback and performance evaluations: Regular feedback and performance evaluations are essential for the growth and development of your HR team. Schedule regular check-ins with each team member to discuss their progress, provide constructive feedback, and set goals for improvement. This feedback should be specific, actionable, and focused on both strengths and areas for development. By providing continuous feedback, you empower your team members to learn and grow.

Lead by example: As a leader, it is important to lead by example and demonstrate the qualities and behaviors you expect from your HR team. This includes being punctual, respectful, and professional in your interactions, as well as showing integrity and ethical behavior. By modeling the desired characteristics, you inspire your team members to emulate them and create a positive work culture.

Real-world example: Let's say you have a newly hired HR specialist who is responsible for managing the recruitment process. To lead and develop this team member, you can start by clearly defining their role and responsibilities, including the specific tasks and targets they need to achieve. You can provide them with training on recruitment best practices, interview techniques, and candidate assessment methods. Additionally, you can encourage them to attend industry conferences or webinars on talent acquisition. By regularly providing feedback and performance evaluations, you can help them identify areas for improvement and set goals for their professional growth. Lastly, you can recognize their achievements by publicly acknowledging their successful hires or positive feedback from hiring managers. This not only boosts their confidence but also reinforces their effectiveness in the role.

How do you foster a positive company culture?

Answer

Lead by example: Show employees that you value a positive company culture by embodying the values and behaviors you want to see in others.

Communicate openly and transparently: Create a culture of trust and honesty by keeping employees informed about company goals, challenges, and decisions.

Recognize and reward employees: Acknowledge and celebrate the achievements of your employees to foster a sense of belonging and motivation.

Promote work-life balance: Encourage employees to prioritize their well-being by offering flexible work arrangements and promoting a healthy work-life balance.

Provide opportunities for growth and development: Invest in the personal and professional growth of your employees by offering training programs, mentorship, and career advancement opportunities.

Encourage collaboration and teamwork: Foster a culture of collaboration by encouraging employees to work together, share ideas, and support each other.

Create a positive physical work environment: Design a workspace that is comfortable, inspiring, and conducive to productivity and well-being.

Promote diversity and inclusion: Create a culture that values and respects diversity by promoting inclusivity, fairness, and equal opportunities for all employees.

Encourage feedback and continuous improvement: Create channels for employees to provide feedback, suggestions, and ideas for improving the company culture and operations.

Summary: Fostering a positive company culture requires leadership, open communication, recognition, work-life balance, growth opportunities, collaboration, a positive physical work environment, diversity and inclusion, and a culture of feedback and continuous improvement.

Compensation and Benefits

Answer

Compensation and benefits are a crucial aspect of the Human Resources Manager's role. They involve the monetary and non-monetary rewards provided to employees in exchange for their work and contribution to the organization.

Here are some key points related to compensation and benefits:

- **Salary**: The salary is the fixed amount of money paid to employees on a regular basis, usually monthly or biweekly. It is determined based on factors such as job responsibilities, experience, and market rates.
- **Bonuses**: Bonuses are additional payments given to employees based on their performance, achievement of targets, or the overall company's performance. They can be in the form of cash, stock options, or profit-sharing.
- **Incentives**: Incentives are rewards provided to employees to motivate and encourage them to achieve specific goals or targets. They can be in the form of cash, gift cards, or other non-monetary benefits.
- **Benefits**: Benefits encompass a wide range of offerings provided to employees beyond their salary. These can include health insurance, retirement plans, paid time off, employee discounts, and wellness programs.
- **Compensation packages**: Compensation packages are the combination of salary, bonuses, incentives, and benefits offered to employees. They are designed to attract, retain, and motivate employees.

Real-world examples of compensation and benefits could include:

- A company offering a competitive salary, performance-based bonuses, and stock options to its employees.
- Providing comprehensive health insurance coverage and retirement plans to ensure the well-being and financial security of employees.
- Offering flexible work arrangements, such as remote work options or flexible working hours, to promote work-life balance.

To summarize, compensation and benefits are an integral part of the Human Resources Manager's responsibilities. They involve determining fair and competitive salary structures, designing incentive programs, and providing attractive benefits to attract and retain talented employees.

How do you determine salary ranges for different positions?

Answer

Research industry standards: HR managers research salary data for similar positions in the industry to ensure competitiveness.

Consider job responsibilities and requirements: HR managers consider the specific job responsibilities and requirements for each position when determining salary ranges.

Analyze internal factors: HR managers evaluate internal factors such as the company's budget, organizational structure, and pay scales to determine appropriate salary ranges.

Consider external factors: HR managers also consider external factors such as the local job market, cost of living, and economic conditions when determining salary ranges.

Consult with management: HR managers consult with top management to ensure alignment with the company's overall compensation strategy and financial goals.

Review employee performance: HR managers take into account employee performance and qualifications when determining salary ranges.

Consider employee benefits: HR managers also consider the value of employee benefits and perks when determining salary ranges.

Regularly review and update: HR managers regularly review and update salary ranges to ensure they remain competitive and aligned with market conditions.

Real-world example: For example, if an HR manager is determining the salary range for a software engineer position, they would research industry salary data for software engineers, consider the specific job responsibilities and requirements for the position, analyze internal factors such as the company's budget and pay scales, consider external factors such as the local job market and cost of living, consult with management to align with the company's compensation strategy, and take into account employee performance and qualifications.

Can you discuss your experience with benefits administration?

Answer

Yes, I have extensive experience with benefits administration as a Human Resources Manager.

Here are some of the key aspects of my experience:

- I have managed the implementation and administration of various employee benefit programs, including health insurance, retirement plans, and wellness programs.
- I have worked closely with insurance providers and brokers to negotiate competitive rates and ensure the best coverage for employees.
- I have developed and communicated benefit policies and procedures to employees, ensuring they are aware of their options and understand how to access their benefits.
- I have conducted open enrollment sessions and provided one-on-one assistance to employees during the enrollment process to address any questions or concerns.
- I have overseen the management of employee benefit records, including enrollment forms, beneficiary designations, and claims documentation.

- I have worked with payroll to ensure accurate and timely deductions for employee benefits, as well as reconciling and resolving any discrepancies.
- I have provided guidance and support to employees regarding benefit-related inquiries, such as claims issues, coverage questions, and eligibility requirements.

Overall, my experience with benefits administration has allowed me to develop a strong understanding of the complexities involved in managing employee benefits and the importance of clear communication and attention to detail.

How do you ensure competitive and fair compensation practices?

Answer
Conduct market research to gather data on industry compensation trends and benchmarks.

Analyze the data to determine the competitive position of the organization's compensation practices.

Review and update compensation policies and practices to ensure they are aligned with market trends and industry standards.

Establish a formal salary structure that outlines pay ranges for different job levels and positions.

Ensure that the salary structure is fair and equitable, taking into account factors such as job responsibilities, required skills and qualifications, and market value.

Regularly review and adjust the salary structure to maintain competitiveness and address any pay gaps or disparities.

Implement a performance-based compensation system that rewards employees based on their individual performance and contribution to the organization.

Ensure transparency in the compensation process by clearly communicating the criteria and factors used to determine pay.

Provide opportunities for employee feedback and input on compensation practices through surveys, focus groups, or other feedback mechanisms.

Regularly communicate and educate employees about the organization's compensation philosophy, policies, and practices.

Monitor and evaluate the effectiveness of the organization's compensation practices through metrics such as turnover rates, employee satisfaction surveys, and benchmarking against industry peers.

Take corrective actions if any discrepancies or issues are identified to ensure fair and competitive compensation practices.

How do you handle compensation negotiations with employees?

Answer

When handling compensation negotiations with employees, it is important to follow a structured and fair approach. Here are some steps to handle compensation negotiations effectively:

- **Gather relevant information**: Before entering into a negotiation, it is crucial to gather all relevant information about the employee's performance, market benchmarks, and company policies. This will help in making informed decisions during the negotiation process.
- **Set clear objectives**: Clearly define the goals and objectives of the negotiation. This could include factors such as salary increase, bonus structure, or other benefits. Having clear objectives will ensure that both parties understand what they are negotiating for.
- **Listen actively**: During the negotiation process, it is important to actively listen to the employee's concerns, needs, and expectations. This will help in understanding their perspective and finding common ground for negotiation.
- **Present data and facts**: Use real-world examples and data to support your proposed compensation package. This could include market research data, performance metrics, or industry standards. Providing factual information will make the negotiation process more objective and transparent.
- **Discuss options and alternatives**: Explore different options and alternatives to meet the employee's needs within the company's budget constraints. This could include flexible work arrangements, additional training opportunities, or performance-based incentives.
- **Find a win-win solution**: Aim to find a solution that benefits both the employee and the company. This could involve compromises and trade-offs on both sides. It is important to maintain a collaborative and respectful approach throughout the negotiation process.
- **Document the agreement**: Once an agreement is reached, it is crucial to document the terms and conditions of the compensation package. This will ensure clarity and avoid any misunderstandings in the future.

By following these steps, HR managers can handle compensation negotiations in a fair and effective manner.

HR Technology and Analytics

Answer

HR technology refers to the use of various software and systems to manage and automate HR processes and tasks. It includes a wide range of tools and applications, such as HRIS (Human Resource Information System), HRMS (Human Resource Management System), recruitment software, performance management systems, and employee self-service portals.

HR analytics, on the other hand, involves the use of data and statistical analysis to gain insights into HR-related issues and make data-driven decisions. It helps HR managers understand trends, patterns, and correlations in workforce data, such as employee turnover, performance, training needs, and workforce composition. By analyzing this data, HR managers can identify areas for improvement, predict future outcomes, and make informed decisions to optimize HR strategies and processes.

Here are some key points about HR technology and analytics:

- HR technology streamlines and automates HR processes, saving time and reducing administrative burden.
- It allows HR managers to easily track and manage employee data, such as personal information, employment history, performance evaluations, and training records.
- HR technology enables self-service portals, empowering employees to access and update their own information, request time off, and view company policies.
- HR analytics helps HR managers identify patterns and trends in workforce data, enabling them to make data-driven decisions and strategies.
- For example, HR analytics can help identify factors that contribute to high employee turnover, such as lack of training or poor management, and develop targeted retention strategies.
- HR analytics can also help predict future workforce needs and identify skill gaps, allowing HR managers to proactively address talent management and succession planning.

Overall, HR technology and analytics play a crucial role in modern HR management by streamlining processes, improving data accuracy, and enabling data-driven decision-making.

How do you leverage HR technology for better efficiency?

Answer

HR technology can be leveraged to improve efficiency in several ways:

- **Automation of administrative tasks**: HR technology can automate time-consuming administrative tasks such as payroll processing, benefits administration, and employee record management. This frees up HR professionals to focus on more strategic initiatives.
- **Streamlining recruitment and onboarding**: HR technology can streamline the recruitment and onboarding process by automating job postings, applicant tracking, resume screening,

and onboarding paperwork. This reduces manual errors, saves time, and improves the overall candidate experience.

- **Enhanced data management and analytics**: HR technology allows for better data management and analytics, enabling HR professionals to make data-driven decisions. For example, HR analytics tools can provide insights into employee performance, turnover rates, and training needs, helping HR managers identify areas for improvement and develop effective strategies.
- **Improved employee engagement and communication**: HR technology can facilitate better employee engagement and communication. For instance, employee self-service portals can provide employees with easy access to their personal information, benefits, and training resources. Additionally, collaboration tools and social platforms can foster communication and collaboration among employees, enhancing engagement and productivity.
- **Mobile accessibility**: HR technology that is mobile-friendly allows employees and HR professionals to access HR information and complete tasks on the go. This can improve efficiency by enabling remote work, reducing the need for physical paperwork, and providing real-time access to information.

Real-world examples of leveraging HR technology for better efficiency include:

- Implementing an HR information system (HRIS) to automate HR processes and centralize employee data. This eliminates manual data entry, reduces errors, and improves data accuracy and accessibility.
- Adopting an applicant tracking system (ATS) to streamline the recruitment process. An ATS can automate job postings, screen resumes, and track candidate progress, making it easier to identify top candidates and fill positions faster.
- Utilizing a learning management system (LMS) to deliver and track employee training. An LMS can automate training enrollment, deliver online courses, and track employee progress, ensuring employees receive necessary training and reducing administrative burden.

Overall, leveraging HR technology can lead to improved efficiency, reduced costs, and better HR decision-making. By automating administrative tasks, streamlining processes, and utilizing data and analytics, HR professionals can focus on strategic initiatives and contribute to organizational success.

Can you discuss your experience with HR analytics?

Answer

Yes, I have extensive experience with HR analytics in my role as a Human Resources Manager.

I have implemented various HR analytics projects to improve decision-making and optimize HR processes.

Here are some specific examples of my experience with HR analytics:

- Developed a predictive analytics model to identify high-potential employees for succession planning.
- Used data analytics to analyze employee turnover rates and identify key factors contributing to attrition.
- Implemented a talent analytics dashboard to track key HR metrics, such as time-to-fill and cost-per-hire.
- Conducted sentiment analysis of employee surveys to identify areas of improvement and develop targeted action plans.

I believe that HR analytics is crucial in today's data-driven business environment, as it allows HR professionals to make informed decisions based on objective data and insights.

By using HR analytics, organizations can enhance their recruitment and retention strategies, identify skill gaps, and optimize workforce planning.

In summary, my experience with HR analytics includes developing predictive models, analyzing turnover rates, implementing talent analytics dashboards, and conducting sentiment analysis of employee surveys.

I am confident in my ability to leverage HR analytics to drive data-based decision-making and improve HR processes.

How do you use data to inform HR decisions?

Answer
Collect and analyze data on various HR metrics such as employee turnover, retention rates, recruitment costs, and performance evaluations.

Use this data to identify patterns, trends, and areas of concern or improvement.

Make data-driven decisions by using insights from the data to inform HR strategies, policies, and practices.

For example, if the data shows a high turnover rate in a particular department, the HR manager can investigate the root causes and implement strategies to improve employee retention.

Regularly monitor and evaluate the effectiveness of HR initiatives using data to determine their impact and make necessary adjustments.

Present data findings to senior management and other stakeholders to support HR recommendations and justify resource allocation.

Use data to forecast future HR needs and plan for recruitment, training, and development programs.

For instance, if the data predicts a high demand for certain skills in the future, the HR manager can proactively hire and train employees with those skills.

Utilize technology tools and software to collect, analyze, and visualize HR data for better understanding and decision-making.

These tools can provide dashboards, reports, and visual representations of data to facilitate data-driven discussions and presentations.

What HR metrics do you find most valuable?

Answer

Employee turnover rate: This metric measures the percentage of employees who leave the company over a specific period of time. A high turnover rate may indicate a problem with employee satisfaction, company culture, or management practices.

Time to fill a position: This metric measures the average time it takes to fill a vacant position. It helps HR managers track the efficiency of the recruitment and hiring process and identify any bottlenecks that need to be addressed.

Employee engagement: This metric measures the level of employee commitment and satisfaction within the organization. It can be assessed through surveys, feedback sessions, or other means. High employee engagement is often correlated with increased productivity and lower turnover rates.

Cost per hire: This metric calculates the total cost incurred by HR for each new hire. It includes expenses such as recruitment advertising, agency fees, and employee onboarding costs. By tracking the cost per hire, HR managers can identify areas for cost optimization and evaluate the effectiveness of different recruitment strategies.

Training and development investment: This metric measures the amount of money and resources invested in employee training and development programs. It helps HR managers assess the organization's commitment to employee growth and development, which can have a direct impact on employee satisfaction and retention.

Summary: The most valuable HR metrics include employee turnover rate, time to fill a position, employee engagement, cost per hire, and training and development investment. These metrics provide insights into employee satisfaction, recruitment efficiency, cost optimization, and employee growth within the organization.

Change Management

Answer

Change management is the process of planning, implementing, and controlling changes within an organization to ensure smooth transitions and minimize negative impacts.

As a Human Resources Manager, you play a crucial role in change management by supporting and driving organizational change initiatives.

Here are some key points to consider when it comes to change management as a Human Resources Manager:

- **Understand the need for change**: Identify the reasons for change and communicate them to the employees. Explain how the change will benefit the organization and its employees.
- **Create a change management plan**: Develop a detailed plan that outlines the steps, timeline, and resources required for the change. Ensure that the plan is aligned with the organization's goals and objectives.
- **Communicate effectively**: Keep employees informed about the upcoming changes, their impact, and the reasons behind them. Use various communication channels, such as emails, meetings, and presentations, to ensure clear and consistent messaging.
- **Provide training and support**: Offer training programs and resources to help employees adapt to the change. Provide support and guidance throughout the transition period.
- **Address resistance**: Anticipate and address resistance to change. Identify potential barriers and develop strategies to overcome them. Encourage open communication and create a positive and supportive environment.

Real-world example:

Imagine a company that is implementing a new performance management system. As a Human Resources Manager, you would be responsible for managing this change. You would need to communicate the reasons for the change to the employees, create a detailed plan, provide training on how to use the new system, and address any resistance that may arise.

Summary:

Change management is an important aspect of the Human Resources Manager's role. It involves understanding the need for change, creating a detailed plan, communicating effectively, providing training and support, and addressing resistance. By effectively managing change, Human Resources Managers can ensure smooth transitions and help the organization achieve its goals.

How do you support employees through periods of change or uncertainty?

Answer

Communicate regularly and transparently: Provide clear and timely information about the changes or uncertainties employees may be facing. Keep them informed about what is happening, why it is happening, and how it may impact them.

Offer support and resources: Provide employees with the necessary tools, resources, and training to navigate through the changes or uncertainties. This can include training programs, workshops, counseling services, or access to relevant information.

Encourage open communication: Create a safe and inclusive environment where employees feel comfortable expressing their concerns, asking questions, or seeking guidance. Encourage open dialogue and actively listen to their feedback.

Provide clarity and direction: Clearly communicate the goals, expectations, and objectives during periods of change or uncertainty. Help employees understand their roles and responsibilities and provide them with a roadmap for success.

Offer flexibility and support: Recognize that employees may have different needs and reactions during periods of change or uncertainty. Be flexible in accommodating their needs, whether it's offering flexible work arrangements, time off, or providing additional support.

Lead by example: Show empathy, understanding, and resilience as a leader during periods of change or uncertainty. Be visible, accessible, and approachable to support employees and demonstrate a positive attitude towards change.

Acknowledge and celebrate progress: Recognize and celebrate small wins and milestones achieved during periods of change or uncertainty. This can help boost morale, motivate employees, and create a positive work environment.

Provide opportunities for growth: Help employees see change or uncertainty as an opportunity for growth and development. Offer learning and development opportunities, mentorship programs, or projects that allow them to expand their skills and knowledge.

Monitor and address issues: Keep a close eye on employee morale, engagement, and well-being during periods of change or uncertainty. Address any concerns or issues promptly and provide the necessary support or resources to help employees cope.

Can you describe a successful change management initiative you led?

Answer

Yes, I can describe a successful change management initiative that I led as a Human Resources Manager.

The change management initiative involved implementing a new performance management system across the organization.

To successfully implement the change, I followed a structured change management process that included the following steps:

- Clearly defining the objectives and goals of the new performance management system.
- Communicating the need for change to all employees and creating awareness about the benefits of the new system.
- Providing training and support to managers and employees to ensure they understood how to use the new system effectively.
- Creating a feedback loop and regularly assessing the progress of the change initiative.

To make the change initiative more relatable and engaging for employees, I used real-world examples and case studies to demonstrate the positive impact of the new performance management system.

I also organized hands-on exercises and workshops to give employees an opportunity to practice using the new system and address any concerns or questions they had.

To visually aid the change management initiative, I created a clear and concise diagram that outlined the steps involved in the new performance management system and how it aligned with the overall organizational goals.

The diagram included visuals such as flowcharts and timelines to help employees understand the logical progression of the change initiative.

Overall, the change management initiative was a success as it resulted in improved employee performance, increased transparency, and better alignment of individual goals with organizational objectives.

How do you handle resistance to change within the organization?

Answer

Recognize the resistance: The first step in handling resistance to change is to recognize and understand that it exists. This involves identifying the individuals or groups who are resisting the change and understanding their concerns and reasons for resistance.

Communicate the need for change: It is important to effectively communicate the need for change to the employees. This can be done through various channels such as town hall meetings, emails, and one-on-one conversations. The communication should clearly explain the reasons for the change, the benefits it will bring, and address any concerns or fears that employees may have.

Involve employees in the change process: Employees are more likely to support and embrace change if they feel involved and have a sense of ownership. This can be done by involving employees in the decision-making process, seeking their input and feedback, and providing opportunities for them to contribute to the change.

Provide training and support: Resistance to change can often stem from a lack of knowledge or skills required to adapt to the new changes. Therefore, it is important to provide adequate training and support to employees to help them acquire the necessary skills and knowledge.

Address concerns and fears: It is important to address any concerns or fears that employees may have about the change. This can be done through open and honest communication, providing reassurance, and addressing any misconceptions or misunderstandings.

Monitor progress and provide feedback: It is important to monitor the progress of the change and provide regular feedback to employees. This helps to keep employees motivated and engaged, and allows for timely adjustments and interventions if needed.

Celebrate successes: Recognize and celebrate the successes and milestones achieved during the change process. This helps to create a positive and supportive environment and motivates employees to continue embracing the change.

Real-world example: Let's consider a scenario where an organization is implementing a new software system. Some employees may resist this change due to fear of technology or concerns about job security. The HR manager can handle this resistance by first recognizing the individuals who are resisting the change, and then communicating the need for the change. The HR manager can address concerns by providing training and support to help employees adapt to the new system. They can also involve employees in the decision-making process and provide regular feedback to monitor progress and address any issues.

What role does HR play in organizational culture change?

Answer

HR plays a crucial role in organizational culture change as it is responsible for managing and shaping the culture of the company. The HR department is involved in various activities and initiatives that contribute to culture change. Some of the key roles of HR in organizational culture change are:

- **Defining and communicating the desired culture**: HR works with top management to define the desired culture for the organization. They then communicate this vision and values to the employees through various channels such as employee handbooks, town hall meetings, and internal communications.
- **Hiring and onboarding**: HR plays a critical role in hiring individuals who align with the desired culture. They develop hiring processes and assessments that evaluate candidates based on cultural fit. HR also ensures that new employees are properly onboarded and introduced to the organization's culture and values.
- **Training and development**: HR is responsible for providing training and development programs that support culture change. They design and deliver training sessions on topics

such as diversity and inclusion, teamwork, and leadership, which help employees adopt the desired cultural behaviors.

- **Performance management**: HR develops performance management systems that align with the desired culture. They set performance goals and expectations that reflect the desired cultural values. HR also provides feedback and coaching to employees to reinforce cultural behaviors.
- **Rewards and recognition**: HR designs and implements reward and recognition programs that reinforce the desired culture. They ensure that employees who demonstrate the desired cultural behaviors are recognized and rewarded appropriately.
- **Employee engagement**: HR plays a key role in creating an environment where employees feel engaged and motivated to contribute to culture change. They implement initiatives such as employee surveys, feedback mechanisms, and employee resource groups, which help in understanding employee sentiments and addressing their concerns.
- **Change management**: HR leads change management efforts during culture change initiatives. They develop change management strategies, communicate changes effectively, and provide support to employees during the transition period.
- **Monitoring and assessing culture**: HR regularly monitors and assesses the progress of culture change initiatives. They collect data through employee surveys, focus groups, and performance evaluations to measure the impact of culture change and make necessary adjustments.
- **Acting as culture champions**: HR acts as culture champions by role-modeling the desired cultural behaviors. They lead by example and ensure that HR policies and practices align with the desired culture.

Overall, HR plays a critical role in organizational culture change by defining and communicating the desired culture, hiring and onboarding employees who align with the culture, providing training and development programs, managing performance, designing reward and recognition systems, fostering employee engagement, leading change management efforts, monitoring culture, and acting as culture champions.

Workplace Health and Safety

Answer

Workplace health and safety refers to the efforts made by an organization to ensure the well-being and physical safety of its employees.

It involves creating a safe working environment, implementing safety policies and procedures, and providing safety training and resources to employees.

The role of a Human Resources Manager in workplace health and safety includes:

- Ensuring compliance with relevant laws and regulations related to health and safety.
- Developing and implementing safety policies and procedures.
- Conducting regular safety inspections and audits to identify and address potential hazards.
- Providing safety training and resources to employees.
- Investigating and reporting any workplace accidents or incidents.
- Collaborating with other departments to create a culture of safety within the organization.

Real-world example: A Human Resources Manager in a manufacturing company might be responsible for ensuring that all employees are trained on how to properly operate machinery, wearing appropriate protective gear, and following safety protocols to prevent accidents and injuries.

Summary:

Workplace health and safety is a crucial aspect of an organization's responsibilities towards its employees. Human Resources Managers play a vital role in ensuring compliance with safety regulations, developing policies and procedures, conducting inspections, providing training, and fostering a culture of safety.

What measures do you take to ensure a safe work environment?

Answer

Conduct regular safety training sessions for all employees to educate them about potential hazards and safe work practices.

Implement a comprehensive safety program that includes policies, procedures, and guidelines for maintaining a safe work environment.

Conduct regular inspections to identify and address any potential safety hazards or issues.

Provide employees with the necessary personal protective equipment (PPE) for their specific job tasks.

Establish clear emergency response protocols and conduct drills to ensure that employees know how to respond in case of an emergency.

Encourage open communication between employees and management regarding safety concerns or suggestions.

Promote a safety culture by recognizing and rewarding employees who demonstrate a commitment to safety.

Regularly review and update safety policies and procedures to ensure they remain effective and aligned with industry best practices.

Can you discuss your experience with workplace safety programs?

Answer

I have extensive experience in implementing and managing workplace safety programs as a Human Resources Manager. Some of my key experiences include:

Conducting regular safety audits to identify potential hazards and risks in the workplace.

Developing and implementing comprehensive safety policies and procedures, ensuring compliance with local and federal regulations.

Providing training and education to employees on various safety topics, such as emergency response, hazard communication, and ergonomics.

Establishing a safety committee comprising representatives from different departments to promote a culture of safety and continuously improve safety practices.

Collaborating with management and employees to investigate and address safety incidents or near-misses, identifying root causes and implementing corrective actions.

Keeping up-to-date with industry best practices and changes in safety regulations to ensure the organization remains compliant and proactive in addressing safety concerns.

Regularly reviewing and updating the safety program to reflect evolving needs and emerging risks.

Real-world example: In one of my previous roles, I successfully implemented a behavior-based safety program that focused on observing and reinforcing safe behaviors in the workplace. This resulted in a significant reduction in workplace accidents and injuries over time.

Another real-world example: I led the development and implementation of a comprehensive safety training program for a manufacturing company, resulting in improved employee awareness and adherence to safety protocols.

How do you handle employee health and well-being initiatives?

Answer

As a Human Resources Manager, employee health and well-being initiatives are a top priority. Here are the steps I take to handle them:

- **Assess the needs**: I start by conducting surveys or meetings to understand the specific health and well-being needs of the employees. This helps me identify the areas where initiatives are required.
- **Develop a strategy**: Based on the needs assessment, I create a comprehensive strategy that includes a range of initiatives to promote employee health and well-being. This strategy may include fitness programs, mental health support, healthy eating options, and stress management workshops.
- **Collaborate with stakeholders**: I work closely with other departments, such as the facilities team, to implement the initiatives. For example, if we are introducing a fitness program, I collaborate with the facilities team to set up a gym or designate a space for exercise.
- **Communicate and promote**: I ensure that all employees are aware of the initiatives and understand their benefits. I use various communication channels, such as emails, newsletters, and posters, to spread awareness. Additionally, I organize events or campaigns to promote participation and engagement.
- **Evaluate and adapt**: It's important to regularly evaluate the effectiveness of the initiatives and make necessary adjustments. I collect feedback from employees and analyze data to measure the impact of the initiatives. This helps me identify areas for improvement or new initiatives that can be introduced.

By following these steps, I ensure that employee health and well-being initiatives are effectively handled and contribute to a positive work environment.

Real-world example:

In my previous role as a Human Resources Manager, we implemented a wellness program that included weekly yoga classes, healthy snacks in the cafeteria, and mental health support workshops. We saw a significant improvement in employee satisfaction and a decrease in absenteeism rates.

What role does HR play in crisis management?

Answer

HR plays a crucial role in crisis management. They are responsible for ensuring the well-being of employees and the organization during difficult times. Here are some specific roles HR plays in crisis management:

- **Communication**: HR is responsible for effectively communicating with employees during a crisis. They disseminate important information, provide updates, and address concerns to keep employees informed and engaged.
- **Employee support**: HR provides support to employees who may be affected by the crisis. This can include offering counseling services, providing resources for financial assistance, or implementing flexible work arrangements to accommodate personal needs.
- **Policy development**: HR plays a role in developing policies and procedures to handle crises. This includes creating emergency response plans, establishing guidelines for remote work, and implementing safety protocols.
- **Training and education**: HR ensures employees are prepared for potential crises through training and education. This can include conducting drills, providing safety training, or offering workshops on stress management and resilience.
- **Conflict resolution**: During a crisis, tensions and conflicts may arise within the organization. HR acts as a mediator to resolve conflicts and maintain a harmonious work environment.
- **Recovery and resilience**: HR plays a role in the recovery and resilience of the organization after a crisis. This involves assessing the impact of the crisis, implementing strategies for recovery, and supporting employees in rebuilding and adapting to changes.

Global HR Management

Answer
Global HR Management refers to the practice of managing human resources on a global scale, taking into consideration the unique challenges and opportunities presented by an international workforce. It involves developing and implementing strategies and policies that ensure the effective recruitment, development, and retention of employees across different countries and cultures.

Key aspects of Global HR Management include:

- **Talent acquisition**: This involves sourcing and selecting the right candidates for international assignments or positions in different countries. It may require considering factors such as language skills, cultural fit, and legal requirements.
- **Training and development**: Global HR Managers are responsible for designing and delivering training programs that equip employees with the skills and knowledge they need to work effectively in a global context. This may involve cross-cultural training, language training, and technical skills development.
- **Compensation and benefits**: Global HR Managers need to establish competitive compensation and benefits packages that attract and retain international talent. This may involve considering factors such as local market rates, cost of living, and tax implications.
- **Performance management**: Global HR Managers are responsible for implementing performance management systems that align with the organization's global objectives. This may involve setting performance targets, conducting performance evaluations, and providing feedback and coaching to employees.
- **Compliance with local laws and regulations**: Global HR Managers need to stay up-to-date with the laws and regulations of different countries to ensure compliance in areas such as employment contracts, working hours, and employee rights.
- **Employee engagement and retention**: Global HR Managers play a crucial role in creating a positive work environment and fostering employee engagement and loyalty. This may involve implementing employee recognition programs, promoting work-life balance, and providing opportunities for career development.

Real-world example:

Imagine a multinational company with offices in various countries. The Global HR Manager of this company would be responsible for ensuring the smooth functioning of HR operations across different locations. They would need to navigate the complexities of different labor laws, cultural norms, and business practices to recruit and retain the best talent.

Summary:

Global HR Management involves managing human resources on a global scale, including talent acquisition, training and development, compensation and benefits, performance management, compliance with local laws, and employee engagement and retention. It requires a deep understanding of different cultures and the ability to adapt HR strategies to a global context.

How do you handle HR challenges in a global or diverse workforce?

Answer

Recognize and embrace diversity: Understand and value the differences in culture, language, beliefs, and perspectives of employees from different backgrounds.

Promote inclusivity: Create an inclusive work environment where everyone feels valued and respected. Encourage open communication and collaboration between employees of different backgrounds.

Provide cross-cultural training: Offer training programs to help employees understand and appreciate different cultures. This can include language training, cultural sensitivity training, and intercultural communication skills development.

Adapt HR policies and practices: Ensure that HR policies and practices are inclusive and sensitive to the needs of a diverse workforce. For example, provide flexible work arrangements to accommodate different cultural and religious practices.

Address language barriers: Implement language support programs, such as translation services or language classes, to facilitate effective communication among employees who speak different languages.

Address unconscious bias: Train HR and management staff to recognize and address unconscious bias in recruitment, performance evaluations, and decision-making processes.

Establish diversity and inclusion goals: Set measurable goals to promote diversity and inclusion within the organization. Regularly monitor progress and make adjustments as needed.

Engage employee resource groups: Support and encourage the formation of employee resource groups (ERGs) that bring together employees with similar backgrounds or interests. ERGs can provide a platform for networking, support, and idea sharing.

Promote diversity in leadership: Ensure that leadership positions are filled by individuals from diverse backgrounds. This can help create a culture of inclusivity and provide role models for employees from different backgrounds.

Summary:

Handling HR challenges in a global or diverse workforce requires recognizing and embracing diversity, promoting inclusivity, providing cross-cultural training, adapting HR policies and practices, addressing language barriers and unconscious bias, establishing diversity and inclusion goals, engaging employee resource groups, and promoting diversity in leadership.

Can you discuss your experience with international HR issues?

Answer

Throughout my career as a Human Resources Manager, I have gained extensive experience in dealing with international HR issues. Here are some key highlights of my experience:

I have worked with multinational companies that have a global workforce, which has given me exposure to a wide range of international HR challenges and opportunities.

I have a strong understanding of different employment laws, regulations, and cultural practices in various countries, which has helped me navigate international HR issues effectively.

I have successfully managed international recruitment and selection processes, ensuring compliance with local regulations and cultural sensitivities.

I have led global HR teams and implemented strategies to promote diversity and inclusion in the workplace, taking into account the unique cultural and social dynamics of each location.

I have designed and implemented global compensation and benefits programs, considering factors such as cost of living, tax implications, and local market conditions.

I have handled complex international employee relations issues, such as cross-border disputes, cultural conflicts, and global mobility challenges.

I have experience in managing international assignments and expatriate programs, including handling immigration, tax, and relocation issues.

I have conducted global HR audits to ensure compliance with international labor standards and best practices, identifying areas for improvement and implementing necessary changes.

I have developed and delivered training programs on international HR topics, equipping HR professionals and managers with the knowledge and skills to effectively deal with cross-border workforce issues.

Overall, my experience with international HR issues has provided me with a solid foundation in managing the complexities of a global workforce and ensuring HR practices align with local requirements and cultural sensitivities.

How do you ensure cultural sensitivity in HR practices?

Answer

Provide cultural sensitivity training for HR staff to increase their awareness and understanding of different cultures.

Establish a diverse and inclusive workplace by actively recruiting and hiring employees from diverse backgrounds.

Develop and implement policies and procedures that promote cultural sensitivity, such as flexible work schedules to accommodate religious holidays or cultural practices.

Create a safe and respectful work environment where employees feel comfortable expressing their cultural identity and beliefs.

Regularly communicate and engage with employees to understand their needs and concerns related to cultural sensitivity.

Offer support and resources for employees to celebrate and share their cultural traditions and customs.

Address any cultural conflicts or misunderstandings promptly and effectively through open communication and mediation.

Regularly review and update HR practices to ensure they align with cultural sensitivity principles and best practices.

Collaborate with diversity and inclusion experts or consult external resources to gain insights and guidance on cultural sensitivity in HR practices.

How do you manage HR policies across different countries?

Answer

Establish a global HR policy framework: Develop a comprehensive set of HR policies that align with the organization's values and goals. These policies should be applicable to all countries while considering local laws and cultural differences.

Customize policies to local needs: Adapt the global HR policies to meet the specific requirements and regulations of each country. This may involve tailoring compensation and benefits packages, working hours, leave policies, and performance management systems to comply with local laws and cultural norms.

Ensure compliance with local laws: Stay up to date with the employment laws and regulations of each country where the organization operates. HR policies should be reviewed and updated regularly to ensure compliance and mitigate legal risks.

Communicate and train: Effective communication is key to ensure that employees across different countries understand the HR policies and their implications. Conduct training sessions, workshops, and provide access to online resources to educate employees about the policies and their application.

Establish a global HR team: Assign HR representatives or a dedicated global HR team to manage HR policies across different countries. This team should have a deep understanding of local laws and regulations and be responsible for implementing, monitoring, and updating policies.

Regularly review and evaluate: HR policies should be regularly reviewed to assess their effectiveness and relevance. Feedback from employees and HR teams in different countries should be taken into account to identify areas for improvement or modifications.

Real-world example: A multinational company has operations in the United States, Germany, and China. To manage HR policies across these countries, the company establishes a global HR policy framework that sets out the overarching principles and guidelines for all employees. However, the policies are customized to meet the specific requirements of each country. For example, the compensation and benefits packages are adapted to comply with local laws and market practices. The company also ensures compliance with local laws by regularly reviewing and updating the policies based on changes in regulations. The global HR team communicates the policies to employees through training sessions and provides ongoing support and guidance.

Ethical Decision-Making

Answer

Ethical decision-making is a process that involves considering ethical principles and values when making decisions. This process helps individuals and organizations determine the right course of action and make choices that align with their ethical beliefs.

Here are some key points to consider in ethical decision-making:

- **Identify the ethical issue**: Start by clearly identifying the ethical issue at hand. This may involve examining the potential consequences of different actions and considering the impact on stakeholders.
- **Gather information**: Collect all relevant information about the situation, including facts, data, and any applicable laws or regulations.
- **Consider different perspectives**: Take into account the perspectives of all individuals or groups who may be affected by the decision. This may include employees, customers, shareholders, and the broader community.
- **Evaluate options**: Generate and evaluate different options for addressing the ethical issue. Consider the potential benefits and drawbacks of each option, as well as how they align with ethical principles.
- **Make a decision**: Based on the evaluation of options, make a decision that is ethically sound and aligns with organizational values. Document the decision-making process and the rationale behind the chosen course of action.
- **Implement and monitor**: Once a decision has been made, put it into action and monitor its outcomes. Regularly assess the impact of the decision and make adjustments as necessary.

Real-world examples of ethical decision-making in a Human Resources Manager role could include:

- **Addressing a conflict of interest**: A Human Resources Manager may be faced with a situation where they have a personal relationship with a candidate applying for a job. In this case, they would need to ethically handle the conflict of interest by ensuring a fair and unbiased selection process.
- **Handling employee complaints**: When an employee raises a complaint about another employee or a workplace issue, the Human Resources Manager needs to ethically investigate the matter, maintain confidentiality, and take appropriate action to address the complaint.
- **Ensuring equal opportunities**: Human Resources Managers play a crucial role in promoting diversity and inclusion in the workplace. They must make ethical decisions to ensure equal opportunities for all employees, regardless of their race, gender, or other protected characteristics.

Summary:

Ethical decision-making is an important aspect of the role of a Human Resources Manager. It involves identifying ethical issues, gathering information, considering different perspectives, evaluating options, making a decision, implementing it, and monitoring its outcomes. Real-world examples of ethical decision-making in this role include addressing conflicts of interest, handling employee complaints, and ensuring equal opportunities.

Can you describe a situation where you faced an ethical dilemma in HR?

Answer

As a Human Resources Manager, I have encountered several situations where I had to navigate through ethical dilemmas. One particular scenario stands out:

During the recruitment process for a key position in our organization, I received two equally qualified candidates. Candidate A was an internal employee who had been with the company for several years and had a good track record. Candidate B was an external candidate with extensive experience in the industry. Both candidates performed exceptionally well during the interviews, making it difficult to choose one over the other.

The ethical dilemma arose when I discovered that Candidate A was a close relative of one of the senior executives in the company. This raised concerns about favoritism and nepotism, which goes against our company's values of fairness and equal opportunity.

On the other hand, hiring Candidate B solely based on their external experience could be seen as disregarding the loyalty and dedication of an internal employee who had invested years in the company.

To address this ethical dilemma, I took the following steps:

- Consulted with the senior executives to make them aware of the situation and any potential conflicts of interest.
- Conducted a thorough assessment of both candidates' qualifications, skills, and fit for the role, ensuring an objective evaluation.
- Established a panel of interviewers from different departments who were not directly involved in the decision-making process to provide unbiased perspectives.
- Documented the entire decision-making process, including the rationale behind the final selection.
- Communicated the decision to all stakeholders involved, emphasizing the objective evaluation process and the importance of maintaining fairness and equal opportunity.

In the end, we decided to hire Candidate A, the internal employee, as they had the necessary qualifications and skills for the role. However, it was crucial to address the concerns of favoritism by ensuring a transparent and fair selection process.

This situation highlighted the importance of maintaining ethical standards in HR and making decisions that align with the organization's values and principles. It also emphasized the significance of documenting the decision-making process to provide transparency and accountability.

In summary, the situation involved an ethical dilemma of choosing between an internal employee with a close relationship to a senior executive and an external candidate with extensive industry experience. I addressed the dilemma by consulting with senior executives, conducting an objective evaluation, involving unbiased interviewers, documenting the process, and communicating the decision transparently.

How do you handle confidential information ethically?

Answer

Maintain confidentiality: As a human resources manager, it is crucial to understand the importance of maintaining confidentiality when handling sensitive information. This includes personal employee data, company financial information, and any other confidential information that may be shared with you in the course of your work.

Adhere to legal and ethical guidelines: It is essential to be familiar with and comply with all applicable laws and regulations related to the handling of confidential information. This includes laws such as the General Data Protection Regulation (GDPR) and the Health Insurance Portability and Accountability Act (HIPAA). Additionally, it is important to follow ethical guidelines set by professional organizations such as the Society for Human Resource Management (SHRM).

Limit access to confidential information: Only individuals who have a legitimate need to access confidential information should be granted permission. This helps minimize the risk of unauthorized disclosure or misuse of sensitive data. Implementing strict access controls, such as password-protected systems and restricted physical access to confidential files, can help ensure information remains secure.

Use secure communication channels: When transmitting confidential information, it is important to use secure communication channels to protect against unauthorized interception. This may include using encrypted email systems or secure file transfer protocols. Avoid discussing confidential information in public or unsecured environments.

Educate and train employees: It is crucial to provide ongoing education and training to employees regarding the importance of handling confidential information ethically. This can include training on data protection policies and procedures, as well as raising awareness about potential risks and best practices for maintaining confidentiality.

Real-world example: For example, if an employee comes to you with a personal issue that they want to keep confidential, it is your responsibility to respect their privacy and keep the information confidential. This may involve not discussing the issue with other employees or only sharing the necessary information with relevant parties who need to be involved in addressing the issue.

Summarized answer: Ethical handling of confidential information as a human resources manager involves maintaining confidentiality, adhering to legal and ethical guidelines, limiting access to confidential information, using secure communication channels, and providing education and training to employees.

How do you ensure HR practices align with ethical standards?

Answer

Develop a clear code of ethics: Establish a code of ethics that clearly outlines the expected behavior and standards for all HR staff members.

Provide regular training: Conduct regular training sessions to educate HR staff members about ethical practices and provide them with the necessary skills to handle ethical dilemmas.

Create a whistleblower policy: Implement a policy that encourages employees to report unethical behavior without fear of retaliation.

Establish an ethics hotline: Set up a confidential hotline where employees can report ethical concerns anonymously.

Conduct regular audits: Regularly review HR practices and policies to identify any potential ethical issues and take corrective action.

Lead by example: HR managers should demonstrate ethical behavior in all their actions and decisions.

Real-world example: For example, an HR manager could ensure ethical standards are being met by implementing a strict policy against discrimination and harassment in the workplace. They could provide training sessions on diversity and inclusion, establish a reporting system for any incidents, and take appropriate action to address and prevent such behavior.

How do you foster an ethical culture within the HR department?

Answer

Lead by example: As a Human Resources Manager, you must set the tone for ethical behavior. By consistently demonstrating integrity, honesty, and fairness, you can inspire your team to do the same.

Establish a code of ethics: Develop a clear and comprehensive code of ethics that outlines the expected behavior and values within the HR department. Communicate this code to all employees and ensure they understand and adhere to it.

Provide training and education: Conduct regular training sessions and workshops to educate HR employees on ethical principles, values, and best practices. This will enhance their understanding of ethical issues and equip them with the necessary skills to make ethical decisions.

Encourage open communication: Create an environment where employees feel comfortable raising ethical concerns and reporting unethical behavior. Establish channels for anonymous reporting to protect whistleblowers and promote transparency.

Promote accountability: Hold HR employees accountable for their actions and decisions. Recognize and reward ethical behavior, and take appropriate disciplinary action when necessary.

Implement ethical policies and procedures: Develop and enforce policies and procedures that promote ethical behavior. This includes fair hiring practices, non-discriminatory policies, and confidentiality measures.

Regularly assess and evaluate: Continuously monitor and evaluate the ethical climate within the HR department. Conduct regular audits and assessments to identify any areas of improvement or potential ethical breaches.

Real-world example: In a real-world scenario, an HR Manager could create an annual ethics training program for all HR employees. This training program could cover topics such as conflict of interest, confidentiality, and handling sensitive employee information. The HR Manager could also establish an anonymous reporting system and communicate its availability to all employees, encouraging them to report any ethical concerns or violations they may witness.

Summarized: To foster an ethical culture within the HR department, lead by example, establish a code of ethics, provide training and education, encourage open communication, promote accountability, implement ethical policies and procedures, regularly assess and evaluate, and provide real-world examples and scenarios to reinforce ethical behavior.

Employee Engagement

Answer

Employee engagement refers to the extent to which employees are emotionally invested in their work, committed to their organization, and motivated to contribute to its success.

Engaged employees are typically more productive, have higher job satisfaction, and are more likely to stay with an organization for the long term.

There are several factors that contribute to employee engagement:

- **Clear communication**: Providing regular updates, feedback, and opportunities for two-way communication can help employees feel more engaged and connected to their work.
- **Recognition and rewards**: Recognizing and rewarding employees for their efforts and achievements can boost morale and motivation.
- **Career development**: Offering opportunities for growth and development can increase employee engagement by showing employees that their organization values their professional development.
- **Work-life balance**: Supporting work-life balance initiatives, such as flexible work arrangements or wellness programs, can help employees feel more engaged and satisfied with their work.
- **Teamwork and collaboration**: Encouraging teamwork and collaboration can foster a sense of belonging and engagement among employees.

Real-world examples of employee engagement initiatives include:

- **Employee recognition programs**: These programs can involve peer-to-peer recognition, manager recognition, or company-wide recognition events to acknowledge and reward employee contributions.
- **Employee surveys and feedback**: Regularly soliciting feedback from employees through surveys or other means can help identify areas for improvement and give employees a voice in shaping the organization.
- **Employee development programs**: Providing opportunities for employees to develop new skills or take on new challenges can increase their engagement and satisfaction with their work.

In summary, employee engagement is crucial for organizational success and can be fostered through clear communication, recognition and rewards, career development, work-life balance initiatives, and teamwork and collaboration.

What strategies do you use to measure and improve employee engagement?

Answer

Conduct regular employee engagement surveys to gather feedback and measure the level of engagement.

Utilize qualitative and quantitative data from these surveys to identify areas of improvement and develop action plans.

Implement recognition and rewards programs to acknowledge and appreciate employees' contributions.

Promote a culture of open communication and encourage employees to share their ideas and opinions.

Provide opportunities for professional development and training to enhance skills and keep employees engaged.

Offer work-life balance initiatives, such as flexible working hours or remote work options, to support employee well-being.

Encourage team-building activities and foster a positive work environment.

Monitor employee turnover rates and conduct exit interviews to understand reasons for disengagement and make necessary improvements.

Regularly communicate organizational goals and values to align employees' work with the company's mission.

Establish performance management systems that provide constructive feedback and set clear expectations.

Develop career advancement pathways and provide growth opportunities to retain and motivate employees.

Can you discuss a successful employee engagement initiative you led?

Answer

One successful employee engagement initiative I led was the implementation of a monthly recognition program.

This program was designed to acknowledge and reward employees for their hard work and contributions to the company.

The program included the following elements:

- A nomination process where employees could nominate their peers for recognition.
- A monthly recognition ceremony where the winners were announced and awarded with a certificate and gift card.
- A communication plan to promote the program and keep employees informed.

To ensure the success of the initiative, I took the following steps:

- Conducted a survey to gather employee feedback and determine what types of recognition would be most meaningful to them.
- Worked closely with the HR team and senior management to gain support and allocate resources for the program.
- Developed clear guidelines and criteria for nominations to ensure fairness and transparency.
- Created a tracking system to keep record of nominations and winners.

The results of the initiative were highly positive:

- Employee morale and satisfaction increased.
- Employee retention improved.
- Team collaboration and engagement levels went up.
- The program received positive feedback from employees and helped create a culture of appreciation and recognition within the company.

Overall, the successful implementation of this employee engagement initiative helped improve the overall work environment and foster a sense of value and appreciation among employees.

How do you address low morale within a team or department?

Answer
- **Identify the root cause of low morale**: Conduct interviews or surveys to gather feedback from team members and identify the underlying issues causing low morale. These could include lack of recognition, poor communication, high workload, or a toxic work environment.
- **Improve communication**: Create open lines of communication by holding regular team meetings, one-on-one sessions, or setting up anonymous suggestion boxes. Encourage team members to share their concerns and ideas, and actively listen and respond to their feedback.
- **Provide recognition and rewards**: Recognize and appreciate the hard work and achievements of team members. This can be done through verbal praise, public recognition, or even small rewards such as gift cards or extra time off.
- **Foster a positive work environment**: Encourage teamwork, collaboration, and a positive atmosphere within the team or department. This can be achieved through team-building activities, social events, or creating a supportive culture.
- **Address workload and job satisfaction**: Assess the workload and ensure that it is manageable. Provide opportunities for professional growth and development, and involve team members in decision-making processes that affect their work.

- **Lead by example**: Set a positive example as a leader by demonstrating empathy, fairness, and professionalism. Show genuine concern for the well-being and job satisfaction of team members.
- **Seek feedback and continuously improve**: Regularly check in with the team to assess the effectiveness of implemented strategies and make necessary adjustments. Actively seek feedback and involve team members in finding solutions to improve morale.
- **Summary**: To address low morale within a team or department, it is important to first identify the root cause of low morale and then take proactive steps to improve communication, provide recognition and rewards, foster a positive work environment, address workload and job satisfaction, lead by example, and seek feedback for continuous improvement.

How do you foster a sense of belonging and inclusion?

Answer

Create a welcoming and inclusive work environment by promoting open communication and respect among employees.

Encourage employees to share their ideas and perspectives, and actively listen and consider their input.

Implement diversity and inclusion initiatives such as employee resource groups, diversity training programs, and mentorship programs.

Celebrate and recognize the diverse backgrounds, experiences, and achievements of employees.

Provide opportunities for employees to collaborate and work together on projects and initiatives, fostering a sense of teamwork and inclusivity.

Establish clear policies and procedures that promote fairness, equal opportunity, and non-discrimination.

Regularly assess and evaluate the effectiveness of inclusion efforts through employee feedback and engagement surveys, and make necessary adjustments.

Address any instances of discrimination or exclusion promptly and effectively, ensuring a safe and supportive work environment.

Legal and Compliance Knowledge

Answer

As a Human Resources Manager, it is important to have a good understanding of legal and compliance knowledge in order to effectively navigate the legal landscape and ensure that the organization is in compliance with relevant laws and regulations. Some key areas of legal and compliance knowledge for a HR Manager include:

- **Employment laws**: HR Managers should have a deep understanding of employment laws, including anti-discrimination laws, wage and hour laws, and laws related to hiring, termination, and employee rights. They should be able to advise the organization on how to comply with these laws and handle any related legal issues that may arise.
- **Labor relations laws**: HR Managers should also be familiar with labor relations laws, such as those related to union organizing, collective bargaining, and unfair labor practices. They should understand the rights and responsibilities of both employees and employers in these situations.
- **Workplace safety regulations**: HR Managers should have knowledge of workplace safety regulations to ensure that the organization is providing a safe and healthy work environment for employees. This includes understanding occupational health and safety laws, as well as any industry-specific regulations that may apply.
- **Privacy and data protection laws**: In today's digital age, HR Managers must also be aware of privacy and data protection laws. They should know how to handle and protect employee data, both in terms of compliance with laws such as the General Data Protection Regulation (GDPR) and in terms of ensuring employee privacy rights are respected.
- **Ethical standards and codes of conduct**: HR Managers should be familiar with the ethical standards and codes of conduct that apply to their organization. They should understand how to promote and enforce these standards, and how to handle any ethical issues that may arise within the workplace.

Real-world examples of legal and compliance knowledge in action for a HR Manager could include:

- Advising the organization on the legal requirements for hiring and firing employees, including ensuring compliance with anti-discrimination laws and following proper procedures for termination.
- Developing and implementing workplace safety policies and procedures to comply with relevant regulations and ensure employee well-being.
- Reviewing and updating the organization's privacy policies and procedures to ensure compliance with data protection laws and protect employee privacy rights.
- Investigating and addressing ethical issues within the organization, such as allegations of harassment or misconduct.

To summarize, a HR Manager should have a good understanding of legal and compliance knowledge in areas such as employment laws, labor relations laws, workplace safety regulations, privacy and data protection laws, and ethical standards. They should be able to apply this knowledge to advise the organization, develop policies and procedures, and handle any legal or compliance issues that may arise.

How do you ensure the organization complies with labor laws?

Answer

Stay updated with labor laws: Regularly review and stay updated with federal, state, and local labor laws to ensure compliance.

Develop policies and procedures: Create and implement policies and procedures that align with labor laws, covering areas like wages, overtime, discrimination, and harassment.

Train employees and management: Conduct regular training sessions to educate employees and management about labor laws, their rights, and responsibilities.

Monitor and enforce compliance: Regularly monitor the organization's practices and procedures to ensure compliance with labor laws. Implement robust auditing procedures to identify and rectify any non-compliance issues.

Maintain accurate records: Keep detailed records of employee information, payroll, and working hours to demonstrate compliance with labor laws.

Respond to complaints and grievances: Establish a process for employees to report any concerns or violations. Promptly investigate and address complaints to ensure a fair and safe work environment.

Engage legal counsel: Seek guidance from legal professionals specializing in labor laws to ensure the organization's practices align with legal requirements.

Stay informed about industry-specific regulations: Research and understand any industry-specific labor laws or regulations that may apply to the organization.

Monitor changes in labor laws: Stay vigilant about changes in labor laws and update policies, training, and procedures accordingly.

Real-world example: For example, if a labor law mandates a maximum number of working hours per week, the HR manager can implement time tracking systems or scheduling software to monitor and limit employee work hours.

Real-world example: Another example is implementing a comprehensive anti-discrimination and anti-harassment policy that includes training sessions and a clear reporting mechanism.

Real-world example: The HR manager can also ensure compliance by maintaining accurate records of employee wages, benefits, and hours worked, as required by labor laws.

Can you discuss your experience with HR-related legal matters?

Answer

I have extensive experience in dealing with HR-related legal matters. Some examples of my experience include:

Ensuring compliance with employment laws and regulations such as the Fair Labor Standards Act (FLSA), Family and Medical Leave Act (FMLA), and Americans with Disabilities Act (ADA).

Conducting investigations into employee complaints and allegations of misconduct, ensuring that all legal requirements are followed.

Providing guidance and advice to management on legal matters, such as employee terminations, discrimination claims, and workplace accommodations.

Drafting and reviewing employment contracts, policies, and procedures to ensure compliance with applicable laws.

Working closely with legal counsel to resolve complex legal issues and mitigate potential risks to the organization.

Keeping up-to-date with changes in employment laws and regulations to ensure compliance and make necessary adjustments to HR practices.

Summarizing my experience, I have been involved in various aspects of HR-related legal matters, from compliance to investigations and providing legal guidance to management.

How do you handle sensitive issues like harassment or discrimination?

Answer

Take all complaints seriously and conduct a thorough investigation into the matter.

Provide a safe and confidential environment for employees to report any incidents of harassment or discrimination.

Ensure that all employees are aware of the company's policies regarding harassment and discrimination and provide regular training on these topics.

Take immediate action to stop any ongoing harassment or discrimination and prevent it from happening again in the future.

Document all incidents and actions taken to address them for future reference and accountability.

Support the victim and offer resources such as counseling or legal assistance if needed.

Communicate the company's zero-tolerance policy for harassment and discrimination to all employees.

Create a culture of respect and inclusivity by promoting diversity and equality in the workplace.

Regularly review and update the company's policies and procedures to ensure they align with current laws and best practices.

Monitor the workplace for signs of harassment or discrimination and address any issues proactively.

Encourage open communication and provide channels for employees to voice their concerns or provide feedback on the company's policies and practices.

How do you stay informed about changes in employment laws?

Answer
Subscribe to legal publications and newsletters that provide updates on employment laws.

Attend conferences, seminars, and webinars related to employment law.

Participate in professional organizations and networking groups for human resources professionals, which often provide resources and updates on employment laws.

Regularly review government websites and resources, such as the Department of Labor or Equal Employment Opportunity Commission, for updates and changes to employment laws.

Collaborate with legal counsel or consultants who specialize in employment law to ensure understanding of new legislation and compliance requirements.

Engage in continuous education and professional development to stay up-to-date on changes in employment laws.

Benchmark with other HR professionals to share knowledge and insights on changes in employment laws.

Maintain a proactive approach by regularly conducting internal audits and assessments to ensure compliance with employment laws.

Utilize technology and software solutions that provide automated updates and alerts for changes in employment laws.

Establish a system for tracking and documenting changes in employment laws, such as a centralized database or document repository.

Scenario-Based Questions

Answer

Scenario-based questions are a type of interview question that presents candidates with a hypothetical situation and asks them how they would respond or handle it. These questions are often used to assess a candidate's problem-solving skills, decision-making abilities, and ability to think on their feet.

Here are some scenario-based questions that could be asked in an interview for a Human Resources Manager position:

- **Scenario 1**: Your company is experiencing high employee turnover. What steps would you take to address this issue?

Potential answer: I would start by conducting exit interviews with departing employees to understand their reasons for leaving. This information can help identify any underlying issues that need to be addressed. I would also review the company's compensation and benefits packages to ensure they are competitive in the market. Additionally, I would work with managers to provide ongoing training and development opportunities for employees, as well as implement retention strategies such as employee recognition programs.

- **Scenario 2**: An employee has filed a complaint about harassment in the workplace. How would you handle this situation?

Potential answer: First and foremost, I would take the complaint seriously and ensure the employee feels heard and supported. I would initiate an investigation into the allegations, following the company's established procedures. This may involve interviewing the employee who filed the complaint, as well as any witnesses or individuals involved. I would also take appropriate disciplinary action if the allegations are substantiated, and ensure steps are taken to prevent future incidents of harassment.

- **Scenario 3**: A manager has approached you with concerns about an employee's performance. How would you address this issue?

Potential answer: I would start by gathering more information about the employee's performance, including specific examples or incidents that have raised concerns. I would then meet with the employee to discuss the concerns and provide feedback on areas where improvement is needed. Together, we would develop an action plan for addressing the performance issues, which may include additional training or coaching. I would also follow up with the manager to keep them informed of any progress or changes.

These are just a few examples of scenario-based questions that could be asked in an interview for a Human Resources Manager position. The key is to demonstrate your ability to analyze situations, make informed decisions, and effectively communicate and collaborate with employees and managers.

Can you provide an example of a successful HR project you led?

Answer

Yes, I can provide an example of a successful HR project I led. One of the projects I led as an HR Manager was the implementation of a performance management system for a company with 500 employees.

The objective of the project was to create a fair and transparent performance evaluation process that aligns with the company's goals and values. Here are the steps I took to ensure the success of the project:

- **Conducted a thorough needs analysis**: I started by assessing the current performance evaluation process and identifying the pain points and areas for improvement. I also gathered feedback from employees and managers to understand their expectations.
- **Researched and selected a suitable performance management software**: After analyzing various options, I recommended and implemented a cloud-based performance management software that met the company's requirements.
- **Designed and communicated the new performance evaluation process**: I created a clear and user-friendly performance evaluation form that captured both quantitative and qualitative feedback. I also conducted training sessions for managers to ensure they understood the new process.
- **Monitored and evaluated the implementation**: Throughout the project, I closely monitored the progress and gathered feedback from employees and managers. I made adjustments along the way to address any challenges and ensure a smooth implementation.
- **Provided ongoing support and training**: After the implementation, I continued to provide support and training to managers and employees to ensure they were comfortable using the new system. I also conducted regular check-ins to address any issues or concerns.

As a result of this project, the company saw several positive outcomes:

- **Improved employee engagement and satisfaction**: The transparent and fair performance evaluation process increased trust and satisfaction among employees.
- **Clear alignment with company goals**: The new process allowed for better alignment between individual goals and company objectives, leading to improved performance.
- **Enhanced development opportunities**: The performance management system provided a platform for managers to identify and support employee development needs.
- **Data-driven decision-making**: The software generated valuable data and insights that allowed HR and management to make informed decisions about talent development and succession planning.

In summary, the successful implementation of the performance management system resulted in improved employee engagement, better alignment with company goals, enhanced development opportunities, and data-driven decision-making.

How do you handle a situation where an employee alleges discrimination?

Answer

- Take the allegation seriously and create a safe and confidential environment for the employee to discuss their concerns.
- Listen attentively to the employee and gather all relevant information about the alleged discrimination.
- Conduct a thorough investigation into the allegations, ensuring that all parties involved are given an opportunity to provide their side of the story.
- Maintain confidentiality throughout the investigation process to protect the privacy of all individuals involved.
- Review any relevant policies and procedures, as well as applicable laws, to determine if any violations have occurred.
- If discrimination is found to have taken place, take appropriate corrective action, which may include disciplinary measures, training, or policy changes.
- Communicate the outcome of the investigation to the employee who made the allegation, while respecting the privacy of all parties involved.
- Monitor the situation to ensure that the discrimination does not continue and take steps to prevent future occurrences.
- Provide support and resources to the employee who made the allegation, such as counseling services or access to an employee assistance program.
- Document the entire process, including the initial allegation, the investigation, and the actions taken, for future reference or legal purposes.

Can you share an example of a difficult termination you managed?

Answer

One example of a difficult termination I managed was when an employee consistently demonstrated poor performance and had a negative attitude towards their colleagues.

Despite multiple coaching and performance improvement discussions, the employee's behavior did not improve, and it started to affect team morale and productivity.

Before proceeding with the termination, I ensured that all the necessary steps were taken, such as providing clear expectations, documenting performance issues, and offering additional training opportunities.

I also consulted with the legal department to ensure compliance with employment laws and company policies.

During the termination meeting, I maintained a calm and empathetic approach, clearly explaining the reasons for the termination and discussing any available support or resources.

I offered the employee the opportunity to ask questions and provided information about their final paycheck, benefits, and the process for returning company property.

To minimize potential disruptions, I had already prepared a transition plan and communicated it to the team prior to the termination.

After the termination, I ensured that affected team members received support and guidance to maintain productivity and morale.

I also conducted a post-termination review to identify any learnings or improvements that could be made in the future.

How do you prioritize HR tasks and projects when faced with multiple deadlines?

Answer
Assess the urgency and importance of each task or project.

Determine the impact on the organization and its employees.

Consider the resources required for each task or project.

Identify any dependencies or interdependencies between tasks or projects.

Communicate with stakeholders to gather their input and understand their priorities.

Create a prioritization matrix or framework to rank the tasks or projects based on their urgency, importance, impact, and resources required.

Allocate time and resources accordingly.

Regularly review and reassess priorities as new information or deadlines arise.

Delegate tasks or projects to appropriate team members if necessary.

Communication and Presentation Skills

Answer

Communication and presentation skills are crucial for a Human Resources Manager as they need to effectively convey information to employees, managers, and other stakeholders.

Some key aspects of communication and presentation skills for a Human Resources Manager include:

- **Clear and concise communication**: HR managers should be able to effectively articulate their thoughts and ideas in a clear and concise manner. This helps in avoiding any miscommunication or confusion.
- **Active listening**: HR managers should have strong listening skills to fully understand the concerns and queries of employees. This helps in building trust and rapport.
- **Non-verbal communication**: HR managers should be aware of their body language, facial expressions, and tone of voice while communicating. This helps in conveying the right message and maintaining a positive image.
- **Written communication**: HR managers often need to write emails, memos, and other written documents. They should have strong writing skills to ensure clarity and professionalism.
- **Presentation skills**: HR managers may need to conduct training sessions or present information to a group of employees. They should have good presentation skills to engage the audience and deliver information effectively.

A real-world example of effective communication and presentation skills for an HR manager can be seen in their role during employee performance reviews. They need to clearly communicate feedback, discuss areas of improvement, and set goals for the future. By using clear and concise language, active listening, and engaging presentation skills, they can ensure that the employee understands the feedback and feels motivated to work towards improvement.

To summarize, communication and presentation skills are essential for a Human Resources Manager to effectively communicate with employees, managers, and stakeholders. Clear and concise communication, active listening, non-verbal communication, strong written communication, and good presentation skills are all important aspects to focus on.

How do you communicate HR policies and changes to employees?

Answer

Use multiple communication channels to ensure that employees receive the information.

Hold regular meetings to discuss HR policies and changes.

Send out email updates with clear and concise information.

Provide written materials, such as handbooks or manuals, that outline HR policies and changes.

Utilize visual aids, such as infographics or posters, to convey important information.

Offer training sessions or workshops to explain HR policies and changes in detail.

Encourage open communication and feedback from employees to address any concerns or questions.

Utilize the company intranet or online platforms to share HR policies and changes.

Organize town hall meetings or forums where employees can ask questions and discuss HR policies and changes.

Use real-world examples and case studies to illustrate the impact and importance of HR policies and changes.

Ensure that the communication of HR policies and changes is aligned with the company's overall communication strategy.

Can you discuss your experience with HR-related presentations?

Answer

I have extensive experience in delivering HR-related presentations to various audiences.

I have successfully presented on topics such as employee engagement, performance management, and diversity and inclusion.

I use clear and concise language, ensuring that the audience understands the key points and takeaways.

I incorporate real-world examples to make the content relatable and applicable to the audience's experiences.

I use visual aids such as slides, charts, and graphs to enhance understanding and engagement.

I structure my presentations in a logical progression, starting with an introduction and clear objectives, followed by a thorough exploration of the topic, and concluding with a summary and call to action.

I often include hands-on exercises or interactive activities to encourage audience participation and reinforce learning.

I also pay attention to formatting and design, ensuring that the slides are visually appealing and easy to read.

For example, in a presentation on employee engagement, I may include a chart showing the correlation between engagement levels and productivity.

In a presentation on diversity and inclusion, I may include a diagram illustrating the benefits of a diverse workforce.

Overall, my goal is to deliver HR-related presentations that are informative, engaging, and actionable for the audience.

How do you tailor your communication style for different audiences?

Answer

Identify the needs and preferences of the audience: Before communicating with a specific audience, it is important to understand their needs, preferences, and expectations. This can be done by conducting research, gathering information, or asking questions to gain insights into the audience's communication style.

Adapt your language and tone: Once you have identified the needs and preferences of the audience, you can tailor your communication style by adapting your language and tone. This means using appropriate vocabulary, avoiding jargon or technical terms that may not be understood by the audience, and choosing a tone that is suitable for the context.

Use real-world examples: To make your communication more relatable and engaging, use real-world examples that are relevant to the audience's experiences or interests. This can help them better understand and connect with the information you are conveying.

Provide hands-on exercises: Depending on the audience, it can be beneficial to provide hands-on exercises or activities that allow them to apply the information you are sharing. This can help them retain and internalize the information more effectively.

Utilize visual aids: Visual aids such as diagrams, charts, or graphs can be used to enhance understanding and make complex information more accessible. These visual aids can also help capture the audience's attention and improve overall engagement.

Format your communication in an engaging way: The formatting of your communication can also impact how well it is received by different audiences. Consider using headings, subheadings, bullet points, or other formatting techniques that make the information easier to navigate and digest.

Ensure logical progression: When communicating with different audiences, it is important to ensure a logical progression of ideas. This means organizing your information in a way that flows naturally and is easy to follow. Consider using clear objectives or guiding questions to structure your communication.

Summarize key points: At the end of your communication, summarize the key points to reinforce the main takeaways for the audience. This can help them retain and remember the most important information.

Real-world example: Let's say you are delivering a training session on workplace safety to a group of employees. For this audience, you would tailor your communication style by using language that is clear and concise, avoiding technical terms or jargon, and providing real-world examples of safety incidents or best practices. You might also incorporate visual aids such as diagrams of proper safety procedures or charts showing accident statistics to enhance understanding and engagement.

How do you handle difficult conversations with employees or managers?

Answer

Prepare for the conversation by gathering all relevant information and facts.

Choose an appropriate time and place for the conversation, ensuring privacy and minimizing distractions.

Start the conversation by clearly stating the purpose and objectives, setting a positive and respectful tone.

Listen actively to the employee or manager, allowing them to express their thoughts and feelings.

Acknowledge their perspective and show empathy, even if you disagree.

Ask open-ended questions to encourage dialogue and understanding.

Use clear and concise language, avoiding jargon or technical terms.

Offer constructive feedback, focusing on specific behaviors or actions rather than personal attacks.

Collaborate on finding solutions and identifying potential areas for improvement.

Document the conversation and any agreed-upon actions or next steps.

Follow up with the employee or manager to ensure progress and provide ongoing support.

Seek guidance from HR or higher-level management if necessary.

Real-world example: When addressing a performance issue with an employee, I scheduled a meeting in a private room to discuss the concerns. I listened to the employee's perspective, asked probing questions to understand their challenges, and provided specific examples of the performance gaps. Together, we developed an action plan with clear expectations and timelines for improvement. I followed up regularly to provide guidance and support, and the employee successfully improved their performance within the agreed-upon timeframe.

Real-world example: During a difficult conversation with a manager who was exhibiting inappropriate behavior towards their team members, I remained calm and professional. I allowed the manager to express their concerns and frustrations, while also articulating the impact of their actions on the team. We discussed the company's policies and expectations, and I offered resources for improving their leadership skills. By addressing the issue directly and providing guidance, the manager was able to modify their behavior and create a more positive work environment.

Summary: Handling difficult conversations with employees or managers requires preparation, effective communication, active listening, empathy, constructive feedback, collaboration, documentation, and follow-up. Real-world examples demonstrate the application of these strategies in different scenarios.

Employee Retention

Answer

Employee retention refers to the ability of an organization to keep its employees for a longer period of time. It is a critical aspect of human resource management as it directly impacts the organization's productivity, cost-efficiency, and overall work environment.

Here are some strategies that can help HR managers in improving employee retention:

- **Competitive Compensation**: Offering competitive salaries and benefits is crucial for retaining employees. HR managers should conduct regular market research to ensure that the compensation packages are in line with industry standards.
- **Career Development**: Providing opportunities for growth and development is key to retaining employees. HR managers can implement training programs, mentorship initiatives, and career advancement opportunities to help employees progress in their careers within the organization.
- **Work-Life Balance**: Promoting a healthy work-life balance is essential for employee retention. HR managers can introduce flexible work arrangements, such as telecommuting or flexible schedules, to accommodate employees' personal needs.
- **Recognition and Rewards**: Recognizing and rewarding employees for their hard work and achievements can significantly contribute to employee retention. HR managers can implement employee recognition programs, performance-based bonuses, and other incentives to motivate and retain employees.
- **Positive Work Environment**: Creating a positive work environment where employees feel valued, respected, and supported is crucial for employee retention. HR managers can foster a culture of open communication, teamwork, and collaboration to enhance employee satisfaction and loyalty.

Real-world examples of employee retention strategies include:

- Google's employee retention strategy focuses on providing a positive work environment and offering attractive perks and benefits, such as free meals, on-site gyms, and generous parental leave policies.
- Zappos, an online shoe retailer, emphasizes a strong company culture and values employee happiness. They offer new employees a $2,000 bonus to quit if they feel the company is not the right fit, which helps ensure that only committed employees stay.
- Adobe implemented a unique employee recognition program called 'The Founders' Award,' where employees can nominate and reward their colleagues for outstanding contributions. This program helps in boosting employee morale and retention.

In summary, employee retention is a critical aspect of human resource management. HR managers can improve employee retention by offering competitive compensation, providing career development opportunities, promoting work-life balance, recognizing and rewarding employees, and creating a positive work environment.

How do you identify & address factors contributing to employee turnover?

Answer

Regularly conduct exit interviews to gather feedback from departing employees.

Analyze data on employee turnover rates to identify trends and patterns.

Monitor employee satisfaction and engagement levels through surveys and feedback mechanisms.

Identify and address issues related to work-life balance, compensation, career growth opportunities, and organizational culture.

Provide training and development programs to enhance employee skills and increase job satisfaction.

Establish open lines of communication to encourage employees to share concerns and provide suggestions for improvement.

Promote a positive work environment and foster a culture of recognition and appreciation.

Offer competitive compensation and benefits packages to attract and retain top talent.

Implement performance management systems to provide regular feedback and address performance issues.

Provide opportunities for career advancement and growth within the organization.

Create a supportive and inclusive work environment that values diversity and promotes equal opportunities.

Regularly review and update HR policies and practices to ensure they align with employee needs and expectations.

Conduct stay interviews to proactively identify and address factors that may contribute to employee turnover.

Utilize data analytics to identify potential turnover risks and take proactive measures to mitigate them.

Collaborate with managers and supervisors to address issues related to employee turnover and develop strategies for improvement.

Can you discuss a successful employee retention program you implemented?

Answer

Yes, I can discuss a successful employee retention program I implemented.

The employee retention program I implemented was designed to address the needs and expectations of our employees and create a positive work environment that would encourage them to stay with the company.

Here are the key elements of the program:

- **Competitive Compensation and Benefits**: We conducted a thorough market analysis to ensure that our compensation and benefits packages were competitive and aligned with industry standards. This helped in attracting and retaining top talent.
- **Career Development Opportunities**: We implemented a robust career development program that included training, mentoring, and opportunities for advancement. This helped employees see a clear path for growth within the company.
- **Work-Life Balance Initiatives**: We introduced flexible work schedules, remote work options, and wellness programs to help employees achieve a healthy work-life balance. This contributed to higher job satisfaction and reduced turnover.
- **Recognition and Rewards**: We implemented a formal recognition and rewards program to acknowledge and appreciate employees' efforts and achievements. This helped in boosting morale and increasing employee engagement.
- **Effective Communication**: We emphasized open and transparent communication throughout the organization. Regular team meetings, town halls, and feedback sessions were conducted to address any concerns and keep employees informed about company updates and decisions.

Real-world Example: One specific initiative we implemented was a 'Stay Interview' program. Instead of waiting until an employee decides to leave, we proactively scheduled one-on-one meetings with employees to discuss their job satisfaction, career aspirations, and any concerns they may have. This helped us identify potential retention issues early on and take necessary actions to address them.

Summary:

In summary, the successful employee retention program I implemented focused on competitive compensation and benefits, career development opportunities, work-life balance initiatives, recognition and rewards, and effective communication. By addressing the needs and expectations of our employees, we were able to create a positive work environment and reduce turnover.

How do you measure the success of retention strategies?

Answer

Employee turnover rate: One way to measure the success of retention strategies is by calculating the employee turnover rate. This can be done by dividing the number of employees who leave the company by the average number of employees in a given time period. A lower turnover rate indicates that retention strategies are effective in keeping employees with the company.

Employee satisfaction surveys: Conducting regular employee satisfaction surveys can provide valuable insights into the success of retention strategies. By asking employees about their level of satisfaction with their job, work environment, and overall experience with the company, HR managers can gauge whether the implemented strategies are positively impacting employee retention.

Retention rate: Another way to measure the success of retention strategies is by calculating the retention rate. This involves tracking the number of employees who stay with the company over a specific period of time and comparing it to the total number of employees. A higher retention rate indicates that the strategies are effective in keeping employees engaged and committed to the organization.

Performance evaluations: Monitoring employee performance through regular evaluations can also help measure the success of retention strategies. If employees are consistently performing well and meeting or exceeding expectations, it can be an indication that they are satisfied and motivated to stay with the company.

Exit interviews: Conducting exit interviews with employees who are leaving the company can provide valuable feedback on the effectiveness of retention strategies. By asking departing employees about their reasons for leaving and their overall experience with the company, HR managers can identify any areas where improvements can be made to enhance retention rates.

Real-world example: For example, a company that implemented a flexible work schedule as a retention strategy could measure its success by tracking the employee turnover rate before and after the implementation. If the turnover rate decreases after implementing the flexible work schedule, it can be inferred that the strategy is effective in retaining employees.

Summary: The success of retention strategies can be measured through various methods, including calculating the employee turnover rate, conducting employee satisfaction surveys, tracking the retention rate, monitoring employee performance evaluations, and conducting exit interviews. These methods provide valuable insights into the effectiveness of the implemented strategies and help HR managers make informed decisions to improve employee retention.

How do you handle exit interviews and feedback?

Answer

Exit interviews and feedback are important for understanding the reasons behind an employee's departure and for identifying areas for improvement within the organization.

To handle exit interviews and feedback effectively, a Human Resources Manager should follow these steps:

- **Schedule the exit interview**: Set up a time to meet with the departing employee to discuss their experiences, reasons for leaving, and any suggestions they may have. This can be done in person or through a video call, depending on the circumstances.
- **Create a comfortable environment**: Ensure that the interview setting is private and conducive to open and honest communication. Make the departing employee feel heard and valued.
- **Ask open-ended questions**: Use open-ended questions to encourage the employee to share their thoughts and feelings. Examples include: 'What factors contributed to your decision to leave?' and 'What could we have done differently to improve your experience?'
- **Active listening**: Actively listen to the employee's responses and take notes. Show empathy and understanding to create a safe space for them to express their opinions.
- **Maintain confidentiality**: Assure the departing employee that their feedback will be kept confidential unless there are legal or safety concerns that need to be addressed.
- **Thank the employee**: Express gratitude to the departing employee for their time, insights, and contributions to the organization.
- **Analyze feedback**: Review the feedback received during exit interviews to identify patterns or common issues that may need to be addressed. Look for opportunities to improve employee retention and satisfaction.
- **Share feedback with relevant stakeholders**: Share the feedback with the appropriate individuals or teams within the organization who can take action on the suggestions or address any concerns raised.
- **Implement changes**: Use the feedback gathered from exit interviews to make appropriate changes or improvements to policies, procedures, or organizational culture.
- **Follow up with the employee**: If possible, follow up with the departing employee after some time has passed to inform them of any changes made based on their feedback. This demonstrates that their input was valued and can help maintain positive relationships.

By following these steps, a Human Resources Manager can effectively handle exit interviews and feedback, contributing to continuous improvement within the organization.

Innovation in HR

Answer

Innovation in HR refers to the use of new and creative approaches to managing human resources within an organization. It involves finding innovative solutions to challenges and leveraging technology to improve HR processes and practices.

Here are some examples of innovation in HR:

- Use of artificial intelligence (AI) and machine learning algorithms to streamline recruitment processes and identify top talent. For example, AI-powered chatbots can be used to conduct initial job interviews and assess candidates' skills and qualifications.
- Implementation of flexible work arrangements, such as remote work and flexible hours, to attract and retain a diverse and talented workforce. This can improve work-life balance and increase employee satisfaction and productivity.
- Adoption of HR analytics and data-driven decision-making to identify trends and patterns in employee behavior and performance. This can help HR managers make informed decisions about training and development initiatives, performance evaluations, and succession planning.
- Integration of employee self-service portals and mobile apps to empower employees to manage their own HR-related tasks, such as updating personal information, accessing pay stubs, and requesting time off. This improves efficiency and reduces administrative burden on HR staff.
- Implementation of employee wellness programs and initiatives to promote a healthy and engaged workforce. This can include initiatives such as stress management workshops, fitness challenges, and mental health support services.

Overall, innovation in HR is essential for organizations to adapt to the changing needs and expectations of employees and to stay competitive in the fast-paced business environment. By embracing new technologies and creative approaches, HR managers can enhance the employee experience, improve productivity, and drive organizational success.

Can you share an innovative HR practice you've introduced?

Answer

One innovative HR practice I introduced is the use of gamification in employee training and development.

Gamification is the application of game elements and mechanics in non-game contexts to engage and motivate individuals.

By incorporating gamification into our training programs, we have seen increased employee engagement, knowledge retention, and skills development.

Here are some key features of our gamified training program:

- **Points and badges**: Employees earn points and badges for completing training modules or achieving certain milestones. This creates a sense of achievement and competition among employees.
- **Leaderboards**: We display a leaderboard showing the top performers in the training program. This fosters healthy competition and encourages employees to strive for better performance.
- **Levels and rewards**: Employees progress through different levels of training, each offering new challenges and rewards. This keeps employees motivated and interested in the training program.
- **Interactive elements**: We use interactive elements such as quizzes, simulations, and virtual reality experiences to make the training program more engaging and interactive.

Overall, the implementation of gamification in our training programs has proven to be an effective and innovative HR practice that enhances employee engagement and learning outcomes.

How do you stay current with HR trends and innovations?

Answer

Subscribe to industry publications and newsletters to stay updated on the latest HR trends and innovations.

Attend conferences, seminars, and webinars related to HR to learn about new developments and best practices.

Join professional HR associations and networks to connect with other HR professionals and share knowledge and insights.

Participate in online forums and communities focused on HR to engage in discussions and learn from others in the field.

Take advantage of online learning platforms and courses to acquire new skills and knowledge.

Engage in continuous professional development by reading books, articles, and blogs on HR topics.

Network with colleagues and attend industry events to stay informed about emerging trends and innovations.

Seek out mentoring or coaching relationships with experienced HR professionals to gain insights and guidance.

Utilize social media platforms, such as LinkedIn and Twitter, to follow thought leaders and HR influencers who share valuable insights and updates.

Stay updated on relevant laws, regulations, and compliance requirements to ensure HR practices align with legal and ethical standards.

Can you discuss your experience with HR technology implementation?

Answer

I have extensive experience with HR technology implementation, having successfully implemented various HR systems and tools in my previous roles.

Some specific examples of HR technology implementation projects I have led include:

- Implementing an applicant tracking system to streamline the recruitment process and improve efficiency. This involved evaluating and selecting the appropriate software, customizing it to fit our organization's needs, and training staff on how to use it effectively.
- Introducing an employee self-service portal that allowed employees to access and update their personal information, request time off, and view company policies and benefits. This required working closely with IT teams to integrate the portal with our existing HR systems and ensuring data security and privacy.
- Rolling out a performance management software that automated the performance review process, set goals, and tracked employee progress. This involved designing and configuring the software to align with our performance management framework, conducting training sessions for managers and employees, and monitoring the system's effectiveness.

In each of these projects, I followed a logical progression by first understanding the organization's HR processes and pain points, then researching and evaluating various technology solutions, and finally implementing and supporting the chosen system. I ensured that the implementation was user-friendly, supported by clear documentation and training materials, and continuously monitored and improved based on user feedback and system analytics.

Throughout my experience with HR technology implementation, I have always prioritized the needs of the end-users and focused on delivering solutions that improve efficiency, accuracy, and employee experience. I am comfortable working with both off-the-shelf software and custom-developed solutions, and I have a strong understanding of the technical aspects involved in integrating HR systems with other business systems.

Overall, my experience with HR technology implementation has equipped me with the skills and knowledge to effectively assess, select, and implement HR technology solutions that align with an organization's goals and enhance HR processes.

How do you encourage innovation within the HR department?

Answer

Create a culture of innovation: Foster an environment where employees are encouraged to think creatively and bring new ideas to the table.

Recognize and reward innovation: Implement a system that recognizes and rewards employees for their innovative ideas and contributions.

Provide training and resources: Offer training programs and resources to help employees develop their innovative thinking skills.

Encourage collaboration: Facilitate cross-functional collaboration to encourage the exchange of ideas and promote innovative thinking.

Set aside time for innovation: Allocate dedicated time for employees to focus on innovative projects and initiatives.

Promote knowledge sharing: Encourage employees to share their knowledge and experiences with others to foster a culture of learning and innovation.

Embrace technology: Stay updated with the latest HR technology trends and leverage digital tools to streamline HR processes and foster innovation.

Stay informed about industry trends: Stay updated on industry trends and best practices to identify opportunities for innovation within HR practices.

Seek feedback and ideas: Regularly seek feedback from employees and stakeholders to gather insights and ideas for improvement.

Emphasize continuous improvement: Encourage a mindset of continuous improvement and provide opportunities for employees to experiment and learn from failures.

Real-world example: One way to encourage innovation within the HR department is to implement a suggestion box or an online platform where employees can submit their innovative ideas. This can provide a platform for employees to share their ideas and contribute to the overall improvement of HR processes and practices.

Another example is to create a dedicated innovation team within the HR department. This team can be responsible for researching and implementing innovative HR practices, technologies, and strategies.

Prioritization and Time Management

Answer

Prioritization and time management are essential skills for a Human Resources Manager. They help HR managers stay organized, meet deadlines, and effectively manage their workload.

Here are some key strategies for prioritization and time management:

- **Identify and categorize tasks**: HR managers should start by identifying all the tasks they need to complete. They can then categorize them based on urgency, importance, and deadlines. This will help them prioritize their workload and focus on the most critical tasks first.
- **Set clear objectives**: HR managers should have clear objectives for each task. This will help them stay focused and ensure they are working towards a specific goal. Clear objectives also help in measuring progress and evaluating the effectiveness of their time management strategies.
- **Use a time management system**: HR managers can use various time management systems, such as to-do lists, calendars, or project management software. These systems help in organizing tasks, setting deadlines, and tracking progress. They also serve as visual aids to help HR managers visualize their workload and prioritize tasks accordingly.
- **Delegate and outsource**: HR managers should identify tasks that can be delegated to other team members or outsourced to external resources. This allows them to focus on tasks that require their expertise and ensures that all tasks are completed efficiently.
- **Avoid multitasking**: Multitasking can lead to decreased productivity and increased errors. HR managers should prioritize tasks and focus on one task at a time to ensure quality and efficiency.
- **Take breaks and manage energy levels**: HR managers should schedule regular breaks to recharge and avoid burnout. They should also be aware of their energy levels and plan their most demanding tasks when they are most alert and focused.

Real-world examples of prioritization and time management for HR managers include:

- Prioritizing employee onboarding and training activities to ensure new hires have a smooth transition into the company.
- Managing recruitment processes by prioritizing job postings, reviewing resumes, and conducting interviews based on the urgency of the hiring needs.
- Balancing day-to-day HR tasks with long-term strategic initiatives by allocating time and resources accordingly.

In summary, prioritization and time management are crucial skills for HR managers. By identifying and categorizing tasks, setting clear objectives, using time management systems, delegating tasks, avoiding multitasking, and managing energy levels, HR managers can effectively manage their workload and meet deadlines.

How do you prioritize HR tasks with competing deadlines?

Answer

- **Assess the urgency and importance of each task**: Prioritize tasks based on their deadlines and their impact on the organization. Identify tasks that are time-sensitive and have a significant impact on business operations or employee well-being.
- **Break down complex tasks into smaller, manageable steps**: If a task seems overwhelming or time-consuming, break it down into smaller sub-tasks. This allows for better time management and helps in allocating resources accordingly.
- **Communicate with stakeholders**: Engage with stakeholders to understand their expectations and priorities. This helps in aligning HR tasks with the overall organizational goals and ensures that important tasks are given due importance.
- **Use technology and automation**: Leverage HR software and automation tools to streamline repetitive and time-consuming tasks. This frees up time for more critical tasks and helps in meeting deadlines.
- **Delegate tasks**: Identify tasks that can be delegated to other team members or external resources. Delegation helps in distributing workload and ensures that tasks are completed within the given deadlines.
- **Reevaluate and reprioritize**: Regularly review and reassess the priority of tasks based on changing circumstances. This allows for flexibility in managing competing deadlines and ensures that the most critical tasks are addressed first.

Can you discuss a situation where you had to manage a high workload?

Answer

In my previous role as a Human Resources Manager, I encountered a situation where I had to manage a high workload due to a company-wide restructuring.

During this period, my team and I were responsible for handling a variety of tasks and projects simultaneously, including employee onboarding, performance evaluations, and policy updates.

To effectively manage the high workload, I implemented several strategies:

- **Prioritization**: I assessed the urgency and importance of each task and prioritized them accordingly. This allowed me to focus on critical tasks first and ensure that nothing fell through the cracks.
- **Delegation**: I identified tasks that could be assigned to other team members based on their skills and workload. By delegating responsibilities, I was able to lighten my own workload and ensure that tasks were completed efficiently.
- **Time management**: I utilized time management techniques such as setting deadlines, creating to-do lists, and blocking off dedicated time for specific tasks. This helped me stay organized and ensure that I made progress on multiple tasks simultaneously.

- **Communication**: I maintained open and frequent communication with both my team members and stakeholders. This allowed me to provide updates, seek assistance or resources when needed, and ensure that everyone was on the same page.
- **Taking breaks**: I recognized the importance of self-care and taking breaks to recharge. By scheduling short breaks throughout the day, I was able to maintain focus and productivity despite the demanding workload.

Through these strategies, I was able to effectively manage the high workload and ensure that essential HR functions continued smoothly during the restructuring period.

Overall, managing a high workload requires a combination of effective prioritization, delegation, time management, communication, and self-care.

How do you ensure HR processes are efficient and effective?

Answer

To ensure HR processes are efficient and effective, there are several strategies that can be implemented:

- Regularly review and streamline HR processes to eliminate unnecessary steps and bottlenecks.

Example: Conduct a thorough analysis of the recruitment process to identify areas for improvement. This may involve automating certain tasks, such as resume screening, to reduce manual effort and speed up the hiring process.

- Implement technology solutions to automate and streamline HR processes.

Example: Introduce an applicant tracking system (ATS) to automate the recruitment process, reducing the time and effort required to manage job applications and track candidate progress.

- Provide training and development opportunities for HR staff to enhance their skills and knowledge.

Example: Offer seminars or workshops on HR best practices, compliance regulations, and the effective use of HR software tools.

- Establish clear communication channels and feedback mechanisms to ensure HR processes are aligned with the needs of the organization and its employees.

Example: Conduct regular employee surveys to gather feedback on HR processes and identify areas for improvement.

- Continuously monitor and measure HR process performance to identify areas of inefficiency or ineffectiveness.

Example: Use key performance indicators (KPIs) to track metrics such as time-to-fill for job vacancies or employee satisfaction with HR services.

By implementing these strategies, HR managers can ensure that HR processes are efficient and effective, contributing to the overall success of the organization.

How do you handle last-minute HR emergencies?

Answer
Stay calm and assess the situation: The first step in handling last-minute HR emergencies is to stay calm and assess the situation. Panicking or acting impulsively can make the situation worse. Take a deep breath and think about the best course of action.

Prioritize the emergency: Once you have assessed the situation, prioritize the emergency based on its impact and urgency. Determine if it requires immediate attention or if it can be handled in a more structured manner.

Communicate with stakeholders: In an HR emergency, it is important to communicate with all relevant stakeholders. This includes employees, managers, and any other parties involved. Provide clear and concise information about the situation, any temporary measures that may need to be taken, and the plan going forward.

Gather necessary information: To handle the emergency effectively, gather all necessary information related to the situation. This may include employee records, company policies, legal guidelines, or any other relevant documentation.

Take immediate action: Depending on the nature of the emergency, take immediate action to address the issue. This may involve implementing temporary measures, conducting investigations, or involving appropriate authorities if necessary.

Document the process: It is important to document the entire process of handling the HR emergency. This includes the steps taken, decisions made, and any communication that took place. This documentation can be useful for future reference or if any legal issues arise.

Evaluate and learn from the experience: Once the HR emergency has been resolved, take the time to evaluate the situation and learn from the experience. Identify any areas for improvement and implement changes to prevent similar emergencies in the future.

Adaptability and Flexibility

Answer

Adaptability and flexibility are important qualities for a Human Resources Manager as they need to be able to navigate and respond to the ever-changing needs of the organization and its employees. Here are some key points to consider:

- Adaptability allows an HR manager to adjust to new situations, changes in policies, and evolving business needs. It involves being open-minded and willing to learn and adapt to new information and processes.
- Flexibility is the ability to change and adapt to different circumstances and work styles. HR managers often have to work with a diverse group of employees with different needs and preferences, so being flexible in their approach is crucial.
- An adaptable and flexible HR manager can effectively handle unexpected challenges and find creative solutions to problems. They can quickly adjust their strategies and plans to accommodate new developments.
- **Real-world example**: An HR manager may be faced with the sudden departure of a key employee. Being adaptable, they can quickly assess the situation and develop a plan to fill the gap, whether through hiring a new employee, redistributing responsibilities, or outsourcing temporary support.
- **Another real-world example**: An HR manager may need to implement a new performance management system. Being flexible, they can tailor the system to fit the unique needs of the organization and its employees, rather than implementing a one-size-fits-all approach.
- **Hands-on exercises**: HR managers can engage in role-playing scenarios to practice adaptability and flexibility. For example, they can simulate a conflict between employees and devise strategies to resolve the issue while considering different perspectives and needs.
- **Visual aids**: A diagram could be created to illustrate the different factors that HR managers need to adapt to, such as changes in technology, industry trends, and employee demographics. The diagram could show how these factors interact and impact the HR manager's role.
- **Engaging formatting**: The content can be organized using headings, bullet points, and subheadings to make it easy to read and navigate. This helps to convey information clearly and concisely.
- **Logical progression**: The answer should follow a logical flow, starting with an explanation of adaptability and flexibility, moving on to real-world examples, and concluding with practical exercises and visual aids.
- **Clear objectives**: The answer should have a clear objective, which is to explain the importance of adaptability and flexibility for a Human Resources Manager and provide examples and ideas for further exploration.

How do you adapt to changes in HR laws or industry trends?

Answer

Stay updated: Regularly stay updated with the latest HR laws and industry trends by attending seminars, workshops, webinars, and conferences. Keep track of HR resources such as industry publications, websites, and professional organizations.

Research and analyze: Conduct thorough research and analysis to understand the implications of new HR laws or industry trends. Identify how they impact the organization's current HR practices and policies.

Consult experts: Seek advice from HR professionals, lawyers, and consultants who specialize in HR laws and industry trends. They can provide valuable insights and guidance on how to adapt to the changes effectively.

Review and update policies: Review existing HR policies and procedures to ensure compliance with new laws or industry trends. Update them accordingly and communicate the changes to the employees.

Train and educate employees: Provide training and educational programs to employees to help them understand and adapt to the changes. This can include workshops, presentations, or online courses.

Monitor and evaluate: Continuously monitor the implementation of new HR laws or industry trends within the organization. Evaluate the effectiveness of the changes and make necessary adjustments if required.

Can you share an example of when you had to pivot your HR strategy?

Answer

Yes, I can share an example of when I had to pivot my HR strategy.

In my previous role as an HR manager at XYZ Company, we were facing a significant increase in employee turnover.

Upon further investigation, we discovered that the main reason for this turnover was a lack of career development opportunities for our employees.

To address this issue and pivot our HR strategy, we implemented the following steps:

- Conducted employee surveys and interviews to understand their career aspirations and areas of improvement.
- Developed a comprehensive career development program that included mentorship, training programs, and opportunities for internal promotions.
- Created a performance management system that provided ongoing feedback and recognition to employees for their achievements.

- Established a talent acquisition team focused on attracting and recruiting top talent with a strong emphasis on career growth.
- Collaborated with department managers to create individual development plans for each employee, aligning their goals with the company's objectives.

The results of this pivot in our HR strategy were significant:

- Employee turnover decreased by 20% within six months.
- Employee engagement and satisfaction increased, leading to higher productivity levels.
- The company's reputation as an employer of choice improved, attracting top talent from the industry.

In summary, by identifying the root cause of the turnover issue and implementing a comprehensive career development program, we successfully pivoted our HR strategy and achieved positive outcomes for both the employees and the company.

How do you handle unexpected challenges in HR management?

Answer

Identify the challenge: The first step in handling unexpected challenges in HR management is to identify the challenge. This involves being aware of any issues or problems that arise and understanding their impact on the organization and its employees.

Analyze the challenge: Once the challenge has been identified, it is important to analyze it to determine the root cause and potential solutions. This may involve gathering data, conducting interviews, or consulting with other HR professionals or experts.

Develop a plan: Based on the analysis, a plan should be developed to address the challenge. This plan should outline the steps that need to be taken and the resources required to overcome the challenge. It should also consider the potential risks and benefits of each solution.

Implement the plan: After the plan has been developed, it should be put into action. This may involve communicating with employees, making changes to policies or procedures, or providing additional training or support.

Monitor and evaluate: Once the plan has been implemented, it is important to monitor its progress and evaluate its effectiveness. This may involve collecting feedback from employees, reviewing data and metrics, or conducting surveys or assessments.

Make adjustments if needed: If the initial plan is not achieving the desired results, adjustments should be made. This may involve revisiting the analysis phase, seeking input from employees or stakeholders, or making changes to the plan or its implementation.

Real-world example: For example, if a company is experiencing a high turnover rate, the HR manager may identify the challenge as a lack of employee engagement. They would then analyze the issue by conducting employee surveys and interviews to determine the root causes of disengagement. Based on the analysis, they might develop a plan that includes implementing a reward and recognition program, providing opportunities for career development, and improving communication channels. The plan would be implemented, and its progress would be monitored through regular check-ins with employees and tracking turnover rates. If the turnover rate does not decrease as expected, adjustments may be made to the plan, such as increasing the visibility of the reward and recognition program or providing additional training on communication skills.

How do you foster a culture of adaptability within your HR team?

Answer

To foster a culture of adaptability within my HR team, I would implement the following strategies:

- **Encourage open communication and collaboration**: I would create an environment where team members feel comfortable sharing ideas, challenges, and suggestions with one another. This can be done through regular team meetings, brainstorming sessions, and open-door policies.
- **Provide ongoing training and development opportunities**: I would invest in the professional growth of my team members by offering training programs, workshops, and conferences. This would enable them to stay updated with the latest industry trends and develop new skills.
- **Emphasize the importance of continuous learning**: I would promote a mindset of continuous learning and improvement among my team members. This can be achieved by setting clear learning objectives, encouraging self-reflection, and providing constructive feedback.
- **Lead by example**: I would demonstrate adaptability in my own work and decision-making processes. By being open to change and willing to take calculated risks, I would inspire my team members to embrace new ideas and approaches.
- **Recognize and reward adaptability**: I would acknowledge and reward individuals who display adaptability and innovative thinking. This can be done through performance evaluations, incentives, and public recognition.
- **Foster a supportive and inclusive culture**: I would create a culture where diversity and inclusion are valued and celebrated. By embracing different perspectives and ideas, my team members would feel empowered to be creative and adaptable in their roles.
- **Encourage experimentation**: I would encourage my team members to experiment with new ideas and approaches. This can be done through pilot projects, small-scale initiatives, and encouraging a 'fail fast, learn fast' mentality.
- **Regularly review and update processes**: I would regularly review and update HR processes to ensure they remain efficient and effective in a changing business environment. This would involve seeking feedback from team members and stakeholders and implementing necessary changes.

- **Provide resources and support**: I would ensure that my team members have the necessary resources, tools, and support to adapt to changing circumstances. This could include providing access to technology, offering flexible work arrangements, and promoting work-life balance.

Team Collaboration

Answer

Team collaboration is a crucial aspect of a Human Resources Manager's role as it involves working together with colleagues and stakeholders to achieve common goals and objectives.

Here are some key points to consider when it comes to team collaboration:

- **Effective communication**: HR managers need to ensure that there is clear and open communication within the team. This includes providing regular updates, sharing information, and actively listening to team members.
- **Building trust**: Trust is the foundation of successful collaboration. HR managers should focus on building trust among team members by being transparent, reliable, and supportive.
- **Encouraging diversity and inclusion**: HR managers should foster an inclusive environment where all team members feel valued and respected. This includes promoting diversity, embracing different perspectives, and creating a sense of belonging.
- **Setting clear goals and expectations**: HR managers need to set clear goals and expectations for the team. This helps in aligning efforts, measuring progress, and ensuring everyone is on the same page.
- **Promoting teamwork and cooperation**: HR managers should encourage teamwork and cooperation by fostering a collaborative culture. This can be done through team-building activities, promoting cross-functional collaboration, and recognizing and rewarding collaborative efforts.
- **Resolving conflicts**: Conflict is inevitable in any team, and HR managers play a crucial role in resolving conflicts effectively. This involves addressing issues promptly, facilitating open discussions, and finding win-win solutions.

Real-world example:

Let's say an HR manager is working on a project to implement a new performance management system. In order to ensure successful collaboration, the HR manager communicates the project goals and expectations to the team, encourages open discussions to gather input and ideas, assigns specific tasks to team members based on their strengths and expertise, and schedules regular meetings to track progress and address any issues or concerns. By fostering effective team collaboration, the HR manager is able to successfully implement the new system and achieve the desired outcomes.

How do you foster collaboration & teamwork within the HR department?

Answer

Establish clear objectives and goals for the HR department, ensuring that everyone understands the purpose and direction of their work.

Encourage open communication and transparency among team members, creating an environment where everyone feels comfortable sharing ideas, concerns, and feedback.

Promote cross-functional collaboration by organizing regular meetings and brainstorming sessions where employees from different HR teams can come together to discuss challenges and find solutions.

Provide opportunities for skill development and training, both within the HR department and through external resources, to enhance collaboration and teamwork.

Recognize and reward collaborative efforts, such as implementing an employee recognition program or acknowledging team achievements during team meetings or company-wide events.

Lead by example by fostering collaboration within the HR department and demonstrating the value of teamwork through your own actions and interactions with team members.

Create a positive and inclusive work culture that values diversity and encourages collaboration among employees.

Implement technology tools and platforms that facilitate communication and collaboration, such as project management software, team messaging apps, or online collaboration platforms.

Regularly evaluate and assess the effectiveness of collaboration and teamwork within the HR department, seeking feedback from team members and making necessary adjustments or improvements.

Real-world example: In a large multinational company, the HR department implemented a cross-functional project team consisting of members from different HR teams, including recruitment, training, and employee relations. This team was tasked with developing a comprehensive onboarding program for new hires. Through regular meetings, collaboration tools, and shared responsibilities, the team successfully created an onboarding program that incorporated the expertise and input of each HR team, resulting in a more efficient and effective process.

Real-world example: A small HR department in a startup company implemented a weekly team huddle, where all team members would gather to discuss ongoing projects, share updates, and address any challenges or concerns. This regular communication and collaboration helped to align efforts, identify areas for improvement, and foster a sense of teamwork and camaraderie within the department.

Can you share an example of a successful HR team project?

Answer
One example of a successful HR team project is the implementation of a new employee onboarding process.

The HR team recognized that the existing onboarding process was outdated and not meeting the needs of new hires, leading to decreased employee engagement and higher turnover rates.

To address this issue, the HR team conducted a thorough analysis of the current process and identified areas for improvement.

They created a project plan that included the following steps:

- Conducting surveys and interviews with current employees to gather feedback and identify pain points in the onboarding process.
- Researching best practices and benchmarking with other companies to learn from their successes and challenges in onboarding.
- Collaborating with other departments, such as IT and facilities, to ensure a seamless onboarding experience for new hires.
- Designing a new onboarding program that incorporated feedback from employees and aligned with the company's values and culture.
- Developing training materials and resources for managers and new hires to support the onboarding process.
- Implementing the new onboarding program and continuously monitoring and evaluating its effectiveness.

The HR team's efforts resulted in a more streamlined and engaging onboarding experience for new hires.

Employee feedback indicated increased satisfaction with the process, and the company saw a decrease in turnover rates among new employees.

This project demonstrated the HR team's ability to identify and address organizational needs, collaborate with other departments, and implement effective solutions.

It also showcased their commitment to continuous improvement and employee satisfaction.

How do you handle disagreements or conflicts within the HR team?

Answer
Encourage open communication and active listening

Identify the root cause of the conflict

Facilitate a constructive conversation to address the conflict

Encourage compromise and finding common ground

Involve a neutral third party if necessary

Follow up to ensure resolution and prevent future conflicts

How do you build a cohesive HR team?

Answer

Clearly define the team's purpose and objectives to provide a common goal for all team members.

Encourage open communication and collaboration among team members to foster a sense of trust and teamwork. This can be done through regular team meetings, team-building activities, and creating a safe space for sharing ideas and feedback.

Provide opportunities for professional development and growth, such as training programs, workshops, and mentoring, to help team members build their skills and expertise.

Promote diversity and inclusion within the team by actively seeking out and hiring individuals from different backgrounds and perspectives. This can help bring fresh ideas and perspectives to the team.

Establish clear roles and responsibilities for each team member to ensure clarity and accountability. This can be done through job descriptions, performance expectations, and regular performance reviews.

Recognize and reward team members for their contributions and achievements to motivate and inspire them to continue working together towards the team's goals.

Address conflicts and issues within the team in a timely and constructive manner. This can be done through open and honest communication, mediation, and team-building exercises.

Regularly evaluate the team's performance and identify areas for improvement. This can be done through performance metrics, feedback from stakeholders, and self-assessment.

Create an inclusive and positive team culture where all team members feel valued, respected, and supported. This can be achieved through fostering a sense of belonging, promoting work-life balance, and celebrating successes.

Leadership Style

Answer

The leadership style of a Human Resources Manager can vary depending on the organization and the manager's personal preferences. Some common leadership styles that HR managers may adopt include:

- **Transformational leadership**: This style focuses on inspiring and motivating employees to achieve their full potential. HR managers who use this style often lead by example and encourage innovation and growth.
- **Democratic leadership**: This style involves involving employees in decision-making processes and valuing their input. HR managers using this style often seek consensus and collaboration.
- **Servant leadership**: This style emphasizes serving the needs of employees and helping them succeed. HR managers using this style prioritize the well-being and development of their team members.
- **Autocratic leadership**: This style involves making decisions without input from employees and expecting strict adherence to instructions. HR managers using this style often have a more hierarchical and command-oriented approach.

Real-world examples of these leadership styles in action in a Human Resources Manager role include:

- **Transformational leadership**: An HR manager who regularly communicates the company's vision and values to inspire employees and fosters a culture of continuous learning and development.
- **Democratic leadership**: An HR manager who involves employees in the decision-making process for implementing new HR policies and procedures.
- **Servant leadership**: An HR manager who actively supports employees' career growth and provides resources and opportunities for professional development.
- **Autocratic leadership**: An HR manager who strictly enforces HR policies and procedures without seeking input or feedback from employees.

To summarize, the leadership style of a Human Resources Manager can range from transformational and democratic to servant and autocratic, depending on the manager's approach and the organization's needs and culture.

Can you describe your leadership style in HR management?

Answer

My leadership style in HR management is a combination of transformational and democratic leadership.

I believe in motivating and inspiring my team members to reach their full potential and achieve their goals.

I encourage open communication and collaboration, where everyone's ideas and opinions are valued.

I provide guidance and support to my team, and I delegate tasks based on individual strengths and abilities.

I believe in empowering my team members to make decisions and take ownership of their work.

I also believe in fostering a positive and inclusive work environment, where diversity and inclusion are celebrated.

For example, when implementing a new performance management system, I involved the entire team in the decision-making process and sought their input on what would work best for them.

I also provided training and resources to support their understanding and implementation of the system.

To summarize, my leadership style in HR management is transformational and democratic, focused on motivating, empowering, and supporting my team members.

I believe in fostering open communication, collaboration, and a positive work environment.

How do you inspire and motivate your HR team?

Answer
Set clear goals and objectives for the team, ensuring that they understand their role and expectations.

Provide regular feedback and recognition to team members for their achievements and contributions.

Create a positive and inclusive work environment, fostering teamwork and collaboration.

Offer opportunities for professional development and growth, such as training programs or conferences.

Empower team members by involving them in decision-making processes and seeking their input and ideas.

Promote a healthy work-life balance, encouraging work flexibility and offering support when needed.

Lead by example, demonstrating passion, enthusiasm, and a strong work ethic.

Create a culture of open communication, where team members feel comfortable sharing their thoughts and concerns.

Celebrate successes and milestones, such as reaching team targets or completing challenging projects.

Provide resources and tools necessary for the team to perform their jobs effectively.

Offer competitive compensation and benefits packages to attract and retain top talent.

How do you handle situations where your HR team faces challenges?

Answer

Identify the challenge: The first step in handling challenges is to identify and understand the problem. This involves gathering relevant information, speaking with team members, and analyzing the situation.

Develop a plan: Once the challenge has been identified, it is important to develop a plan of action. This plan should outline the steps that need to be taken to address the challenge and resolve it.

Communicate with team members: It is crucial to keep the HR team informed about the challenge and the steps being taken to address it. Regular communication helps in maintaining transparency and building trust.

Provide support and resources: In order to effectively handle challenges, it is important to provide the HR team with the necessary support and resources. This could include additional training, mentoring, or access to tools and technology.

Encourage collaboration: Collaboration within the HR team can help in brainstorming ideas and finding innovative solutions to challenges. Encouraging teamwork and creating a supportive work environment is essential.

Monitor progress: It is important to monitor the progress of the plan and make any necessary adjustments along the way. Regular check-ins and feedback sessions can help in identifying any issues and taking corrective actions.

Evaluate and learn: After the challenge has been resolved, it is important to evaluate the effectiveness of the plan and learn from the experience. This helps in improving future decision-making and handling similar challenges in a better way.

How do you lead HR initiatives with executive buy-in?

Answer

Understand the strategic goals and objectives of the organization and align HR initiatives with them.

Communicate the value and benefits of HR initiatives to executives in a clear and compelling manner.

Provide real-world examples of successful HR initiatives in other organizations to demonstrate the potential impact.

Engage executives in the decision-making process by involving them in the planning and implementation of HR initiatives.

Seek feedback and input from executives to ensure their perspectives are considered and incorporated into the initiatives.

Create a business case for HR initiatives that outlines the expected outcomes and return on investment.

Develop a comprehensive communication plan to keep executives informed about the progress and results of HR initiatives.

Use visual aids such as charts, graphs, and diagrams to present data and information in a clear and engaging way.

Provide hands-on exercises and training opportunities for executives to learn about HR initiatives and their benefits.

Ensure that the formatting of any written materials related to HR initiatives is engaging and easy to read.

Clearly define the objectives and goals of HR initiatives to ensure that executives understand what they are supporting.

Maintain a logical progression in the implementation of HR initiatives, with clear milestones and deadlines.

Professional Development

Answer

Professional development is an essential part of a Human Resources Manager's career. It involves continuously improving their skills, knowledge, and abilities to stay up-to-date with the latest industry trends and best practices.

Here are some key aspects of professional development for a Human Resources Manager:

- **Continuous learning**: HR Managers should actively seek out opportunities to learn and expand their knowledge. This can include attending conferences, workshops, and seminars, as well as participating in online courses and webinars.
- **Networking**: Building a strong professional network can provide HR Managers with valuable connections and resources. They can join HR associations, attend industry events, and engage in online communities to connect with other professionals in their field.
- **Certifications**: Earning relevant certifications can demonstrate HR Managers' expertise and commitment to professional development. Some popular HR certifications include the Professional in Human Resources (PHR) and the Senior Professional in Human Resources (SPHR) certifications.
- **Mentorship**: Seeking guidance from experienced HR professionals can provide valuable insights and help HR Managers grow in their careers. They can seek out mentors within their organization or through professional associations.
- **Leadership development**: HR Managers should focus on developing their leadership skills to effectively manage teams and drive organizational success. This can involve attending leadership training programs, seeking out leadership roles within their organization, and actively practicing leadership principles.

Real-world examples of professional development for a Human Resources Manager could include:

- Attending a conference on the latest trends and best practices in HR management.
- Completing an online course on employment law and compliance.
- Participating in a workshop on conflict resolution and mediation skills.
- Obtaining a certification in recruitment and talent acquisition.

Summarizing, professional development for a Human Resources Manager involves continuous learning, networking, earning certifications, seeking mentorship, and developing leadership skills. It is essential for staying current in the field and advancing in their career.

How do you stay updated on HR best practices and industry trends?

Answer

Read industry publications and HR blogs to stay informed about the latest trends and best practices in the field.

Attend HR conferences and seminars to learn from experts and network with other HR professionals.

Join professional HR associations and participate in their events and webinars to gain insights from industry leaders.

Engage in continuous learning and professional development by taking HR courses and certifications.

Utilize social media platforms like LinkedIn to connect with other HR professionals and follow thought leaders in the industry.

Stay updated on relevant laws and regulations by regularly reviewing legal resources and attending legal seminars.

Seek feedback and advice from mentors or more experienced HR professionals to gain different perspectives and insights.

Participate in HR case studies and discussions to learn from real-world examples and practical experiences.

Subscribe to HR newsletters and email updates to receive regular updates on industry news and best practices.

Collaborate with colleagues in HR and other departments to share knowledge and exchange ideas on HR practices and trends.

Discuss any HR-related certifications or professional development?

Answer

There are several HR-related certifications and professional development opportunities available for individuals in the field of Human Resources. These certifications and programs can help individuals enhance their skills and stay updated with the latest trends and best practices in HR.

Some of the popular HR certifications and professional development programs include:

- **Professional in Human Resources (PHR)**: This certification is offered by the Human Resource Certification Institute (HRCI) and is designed for HR professionals who have experience in the field. It covers various HR functional areas and validates the individual's knowledge and expertise in HR.
- **Senior Professional in Human Resources (SPHR)**: Also offered by HRCI, this certification is for senior-level HR professionals with a higher level of knowledge and experience in HR management.
- **Society for Human Resource Management Certified Professional (SHRM-CP)**: This certification is offered by the Society for Human Resource Management (SHRM) and is designed for HR professionals who are engaged in operational HR activities.

- **Society for Human Resource Management Senior Certified Professional (SHRM-SCP):** This certification, also offered by SHRM, is for senior-level HR professionals who are engaged in strategic HR activities.
- **Certified Compensation Professional (CCP):** This certification is offered by WorldatWork and focuses on compensation and benefits management. It validates the individual's knowledge and expertise in designing and managing compensation programs.

Apart from these certifications, there are also various professional development programs and workshops available for HR professionals. These programs cover a wide range of topics such as employee relations, talent acquisition, performance management, and HR analytics.

Attending these programs and obtaining certifications can help HR professionals demonstrate their commitment to continuous learning and professional development. It can also enhance their credibility and open up new career opportunities in the field of HR.

Summary: HR professionals have the opportunity to enhance their skills and stay updated through various HR-related certifications and professional development programs. These certifications validate their knowledge and expertise in specific HR areas, while professional development programs cover a wide range of HR topics. Attending these programs and obtaining certifications can help HR professionals demonstrate their commitment to continuous learning and professional growth, and open up new career opportunities.

How do you encourage continuous learning within your HR team?

Answer

Establish a learning culture within the HR team by emphasizing the importance of continuous learning and professional development.

Provide opportunities for ongoing training and development through workshops, seminars, conferences, and online courses.

Encourage HR team members to set learning goals and create personalized development plans.

Promote knowledge sharing within the team through regular meetings, discussions, and presentations.

Recognize and reward team members who demonstrate a commitment to continuous learning.

Provide resources such as books, articles, and online resources to support self-directed learning.

Offer mentoring and coaching programs to support the growth and development of team members.

Create a supportive and inclusive environment where team members feel comfortable asking questions and seeking feedback.

Regularly assess and evaluate the effectiveness of the learning initiatives and make improvements as needed.

Where do you see the future of HR, and how do you plan to stay ahead?

Answer

The future of HR is rapidly evolving, and it is crucial for Human Resources Managers to stay ahead of the trends and changes in the field.

Some key areas where I see the future of HR heading are:

- **Technology integration**: HR will continue to leverage technology to streamline processes, improve efficiency, and enhance the employee experience. For example, the use of artificial intelligence in recruitment and employee engagement tools.
- **Data-driven decision making**: HR will increasingly rely on data analytics to make informed decisions. This includes analyzing employee data to identify trends, predict future needs, and measure the impact of HR initiatives.
- **Focus on employee well-being**: The future of HR will prioritize employee well-being and work-life balance. This includes promoting mental health initiatives, flexible work arrangements, and creating a positive work environment.
- **Diversity and inclusion**: HR will play a critical role in fostering diversity and inclusion within organizations. This includes implementing inclusive hiring practices, promoting diversity in leadership roles, and creating a culture of belonging.

To stay ahead in the field of HR, I plan to:

- **Continuously learn and adapt**: I will stay updated with the latest HR trends and best practices by attending conferences, workshops, and participating in professional development programs.
- **Embrace technology**: I will actively seek opportunities to integrate technology into HR processes and stay updated with emerging tools and platforms.
- **Develop data analysis skills**: I will enhance my data analysis skills to effectively leverage data in decision making and to measure the impact of HR initiatives.
- **Foster a culture of well-being**: I will prioritize employee well-being and actively promote initiatives that support work-life balance and mental health.
- **Enhance diversity and inclusion efforts**: I will work towards creating a diverse and inclusive work environment by implementing inclusive hiring practices, providing diversity training, and fostering a culture of belonging.

By staying ahead in these areas, I aim to contribute to the success of the organization and create a positive impact on the employees' experience.